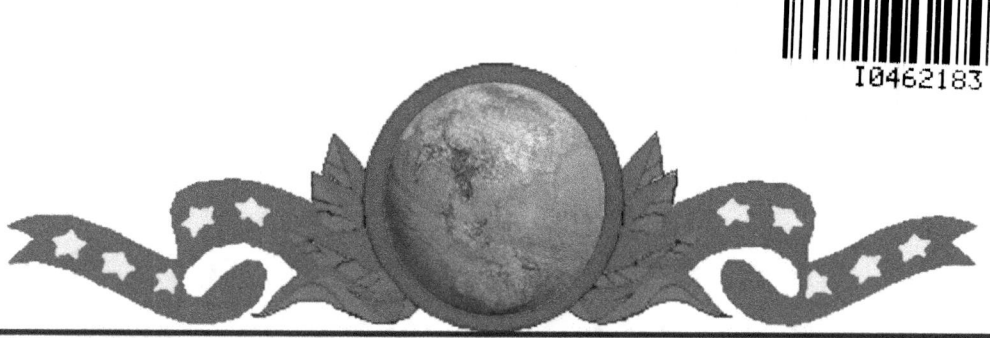

Real World

Colouring Book

For Advanced Users & Adults

Copyright 2019 By John Boom

50 Images

Created From Real Life Photos
For You To Colour As You Please.

ISBN 978-0-359-93584-0

9 780359 935840
90000

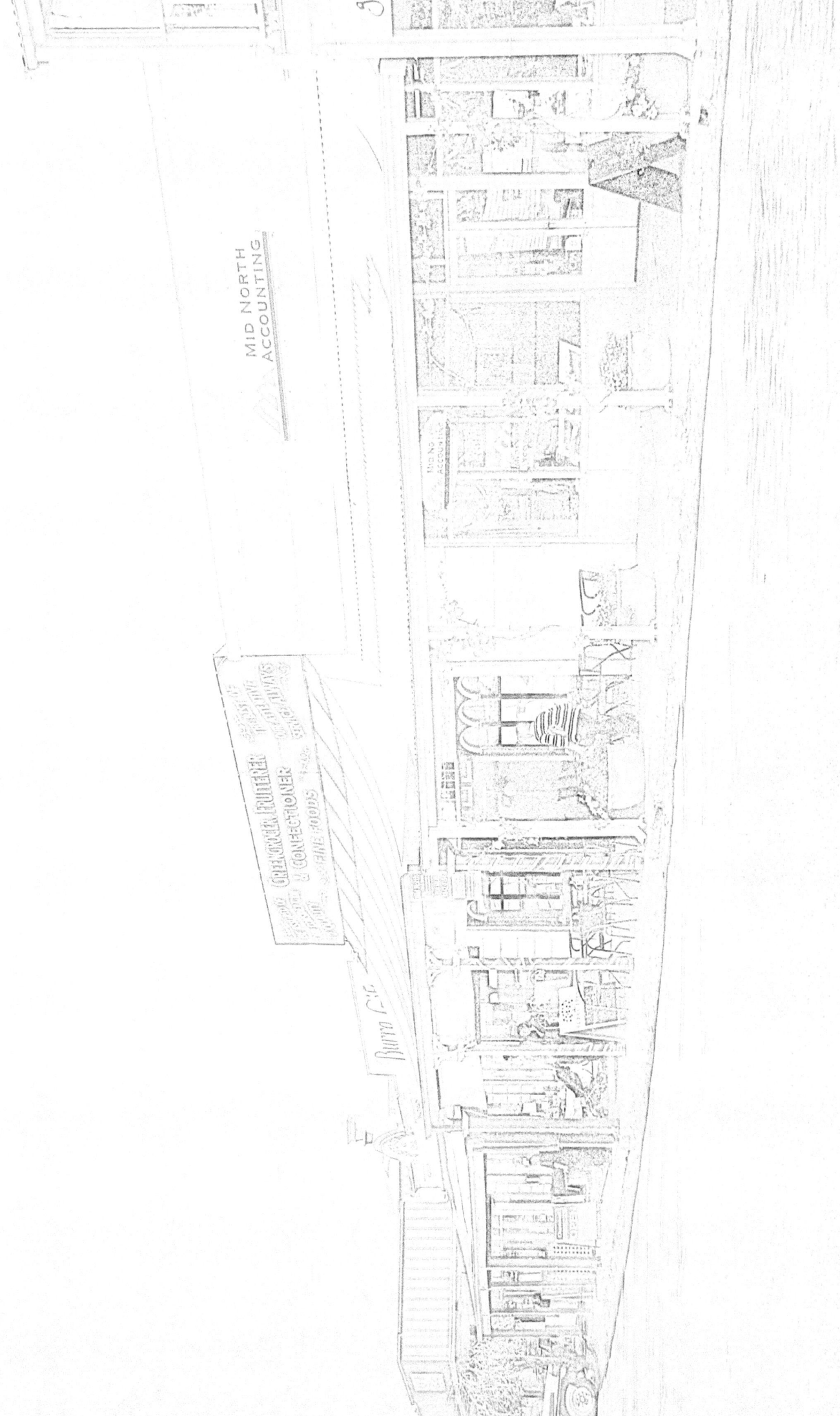

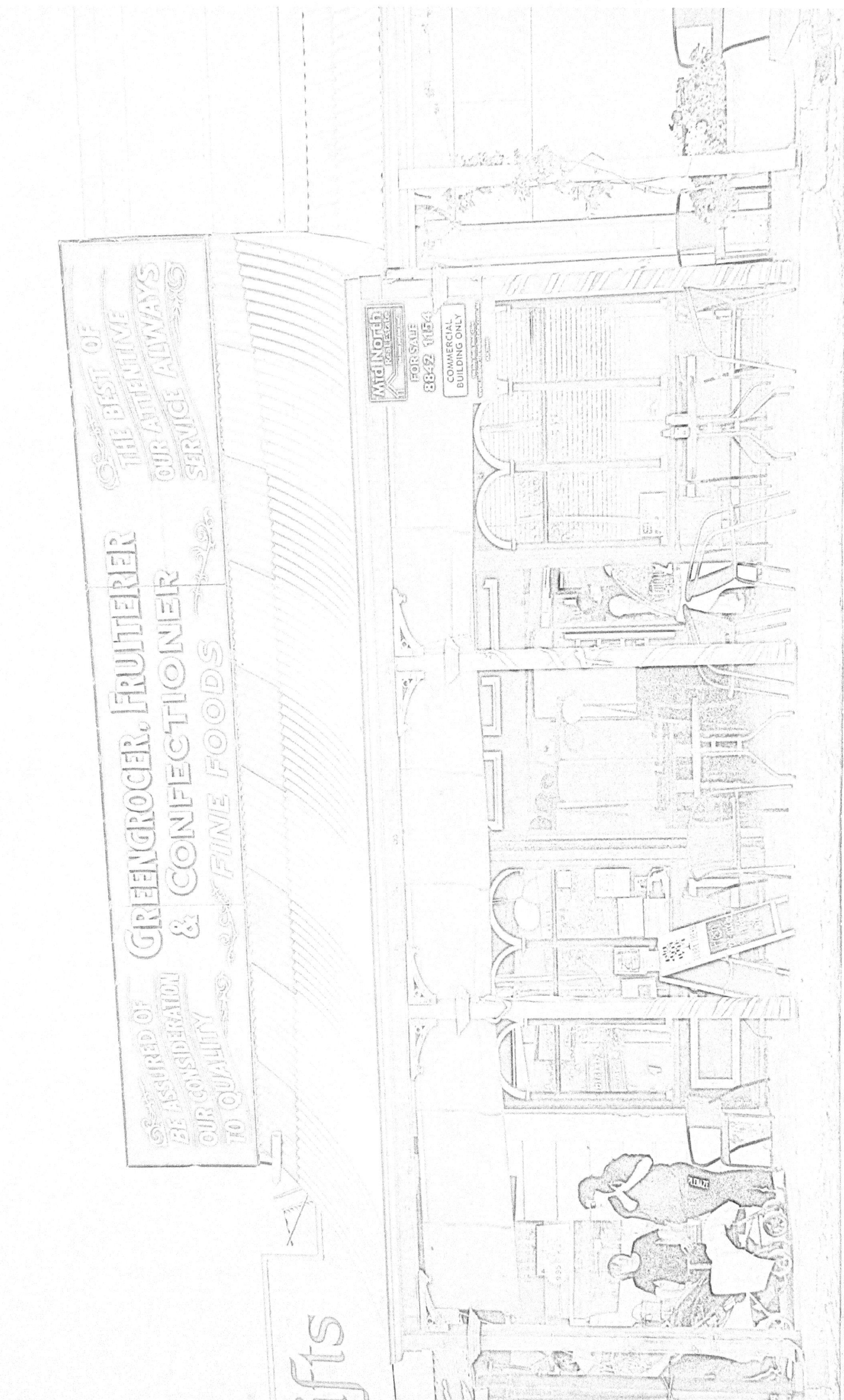

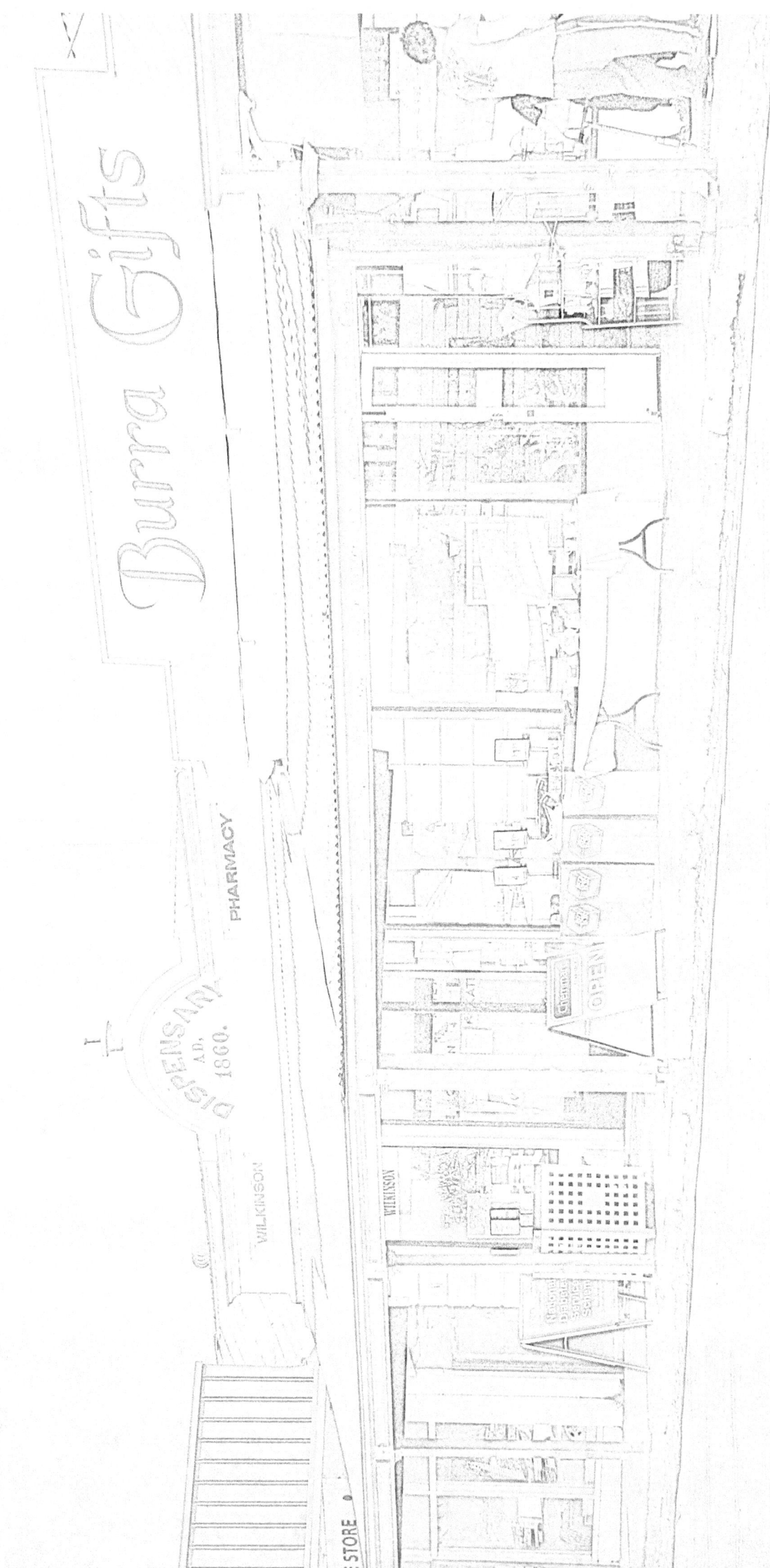

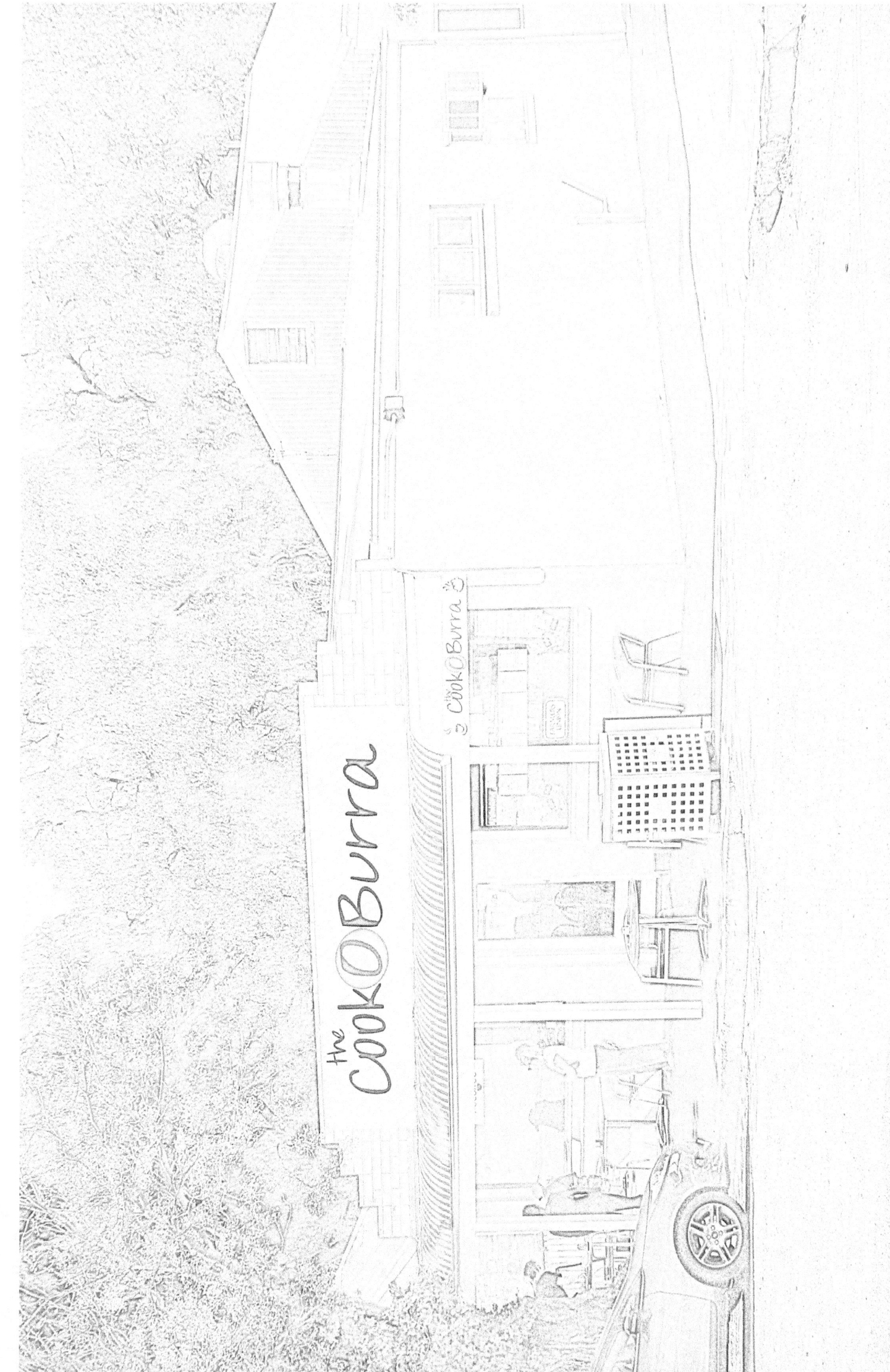

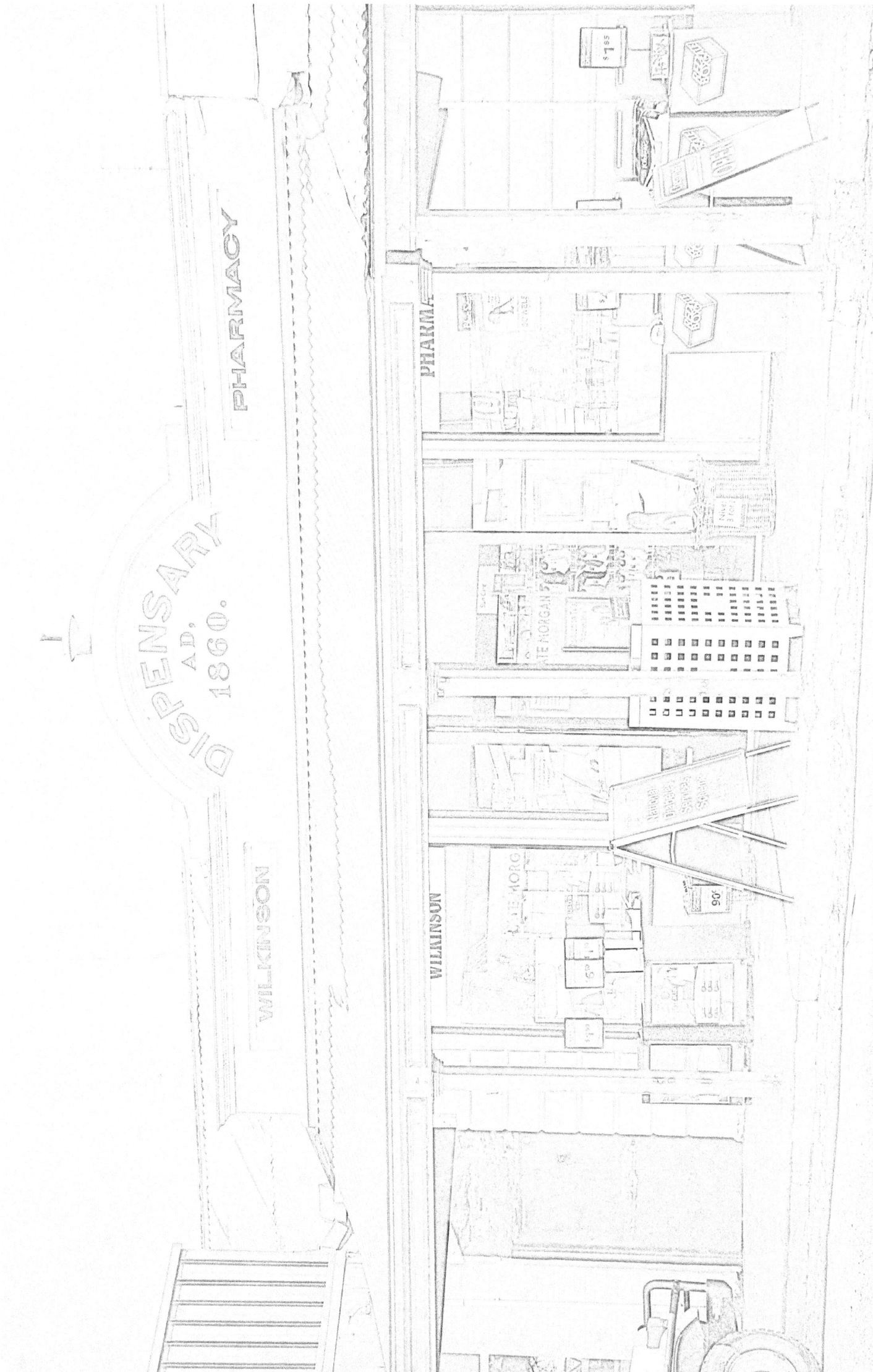

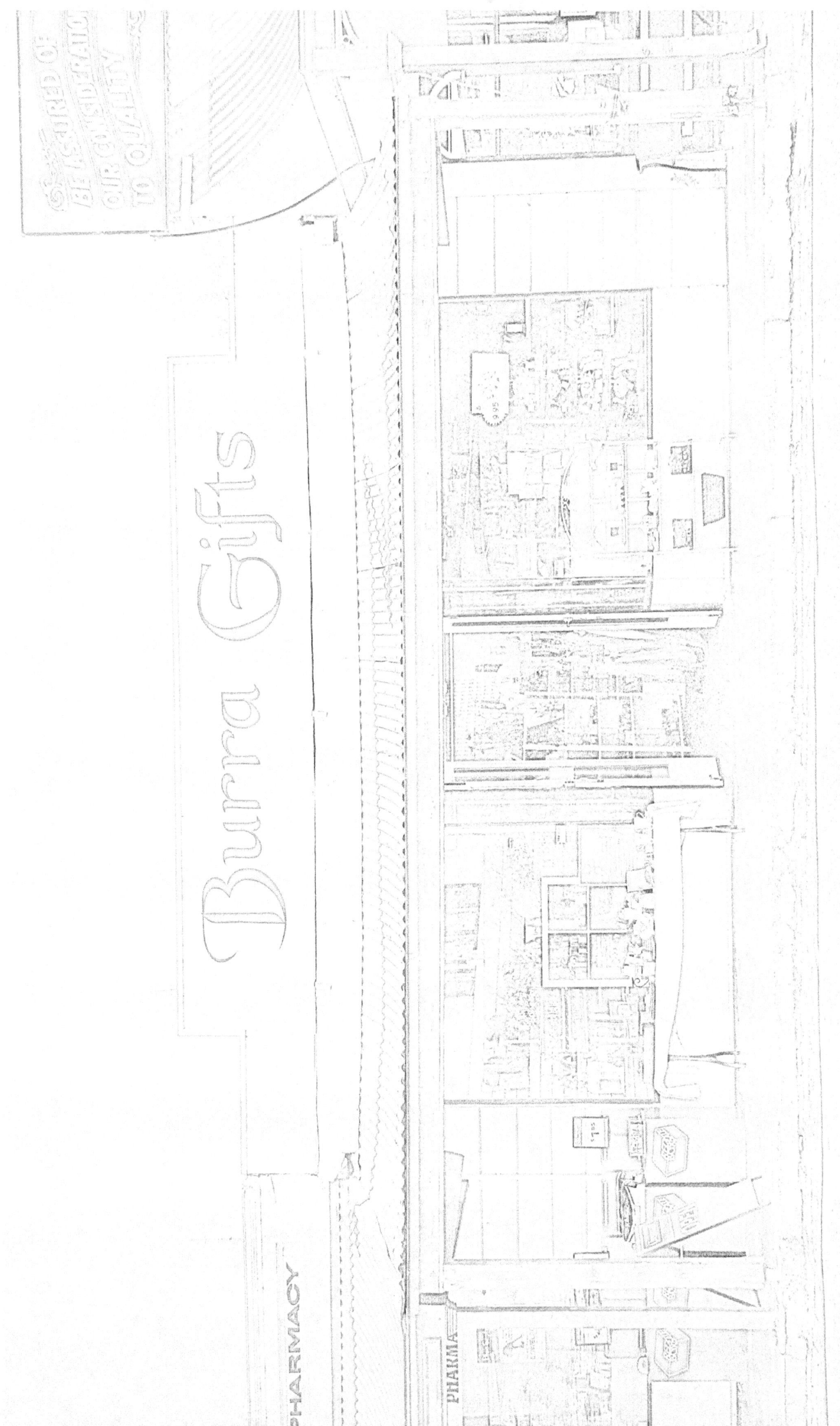

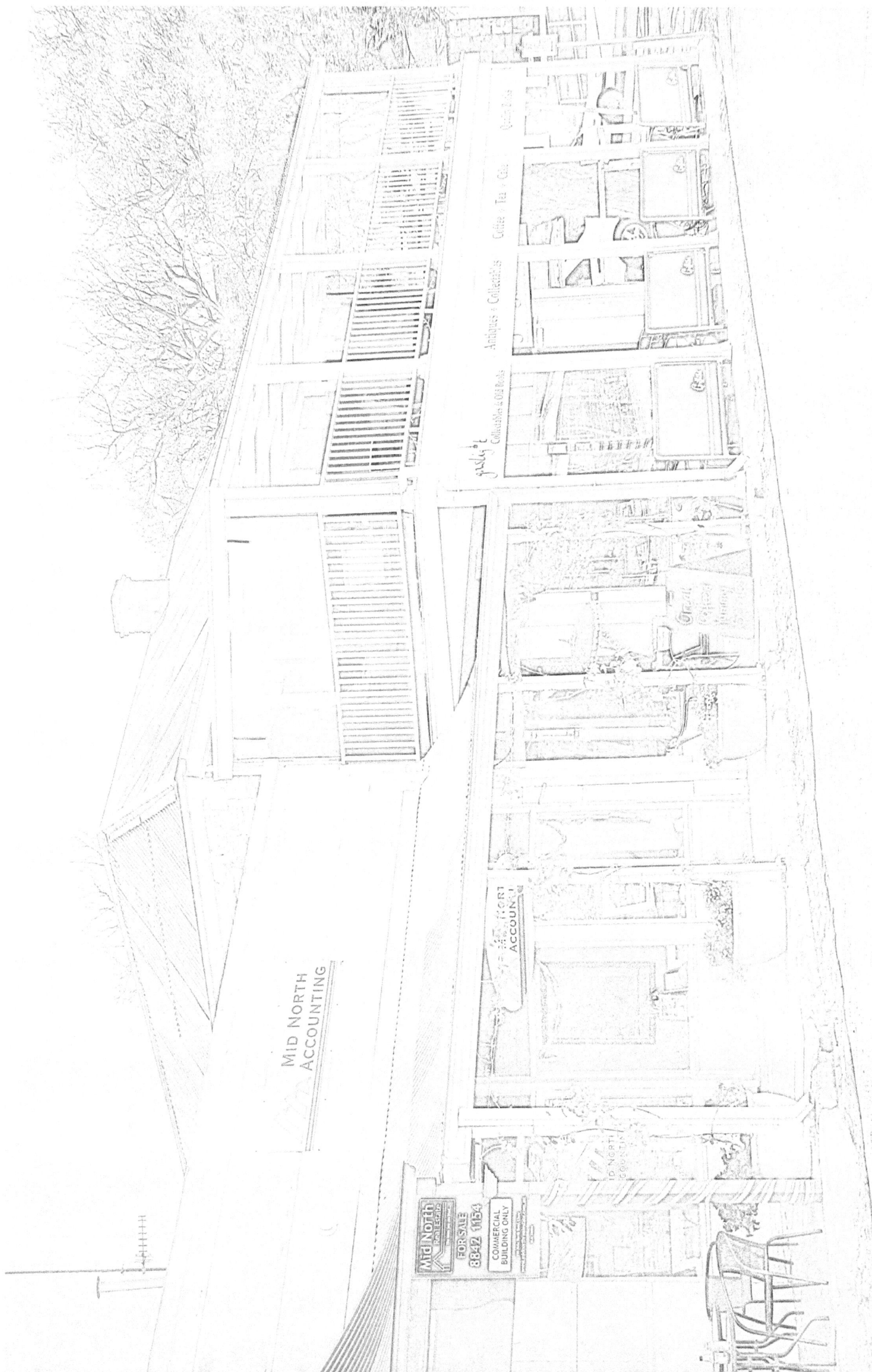

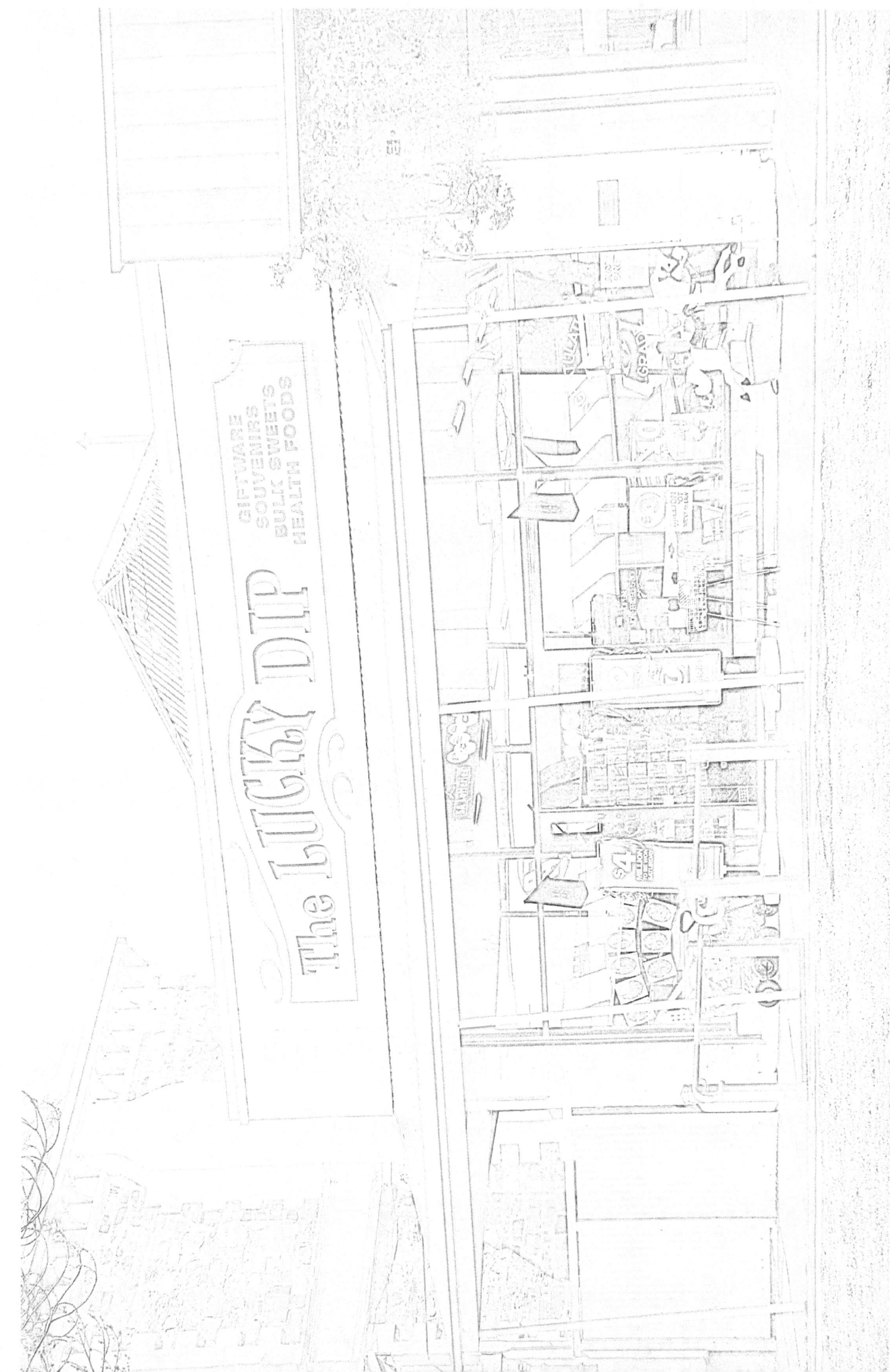

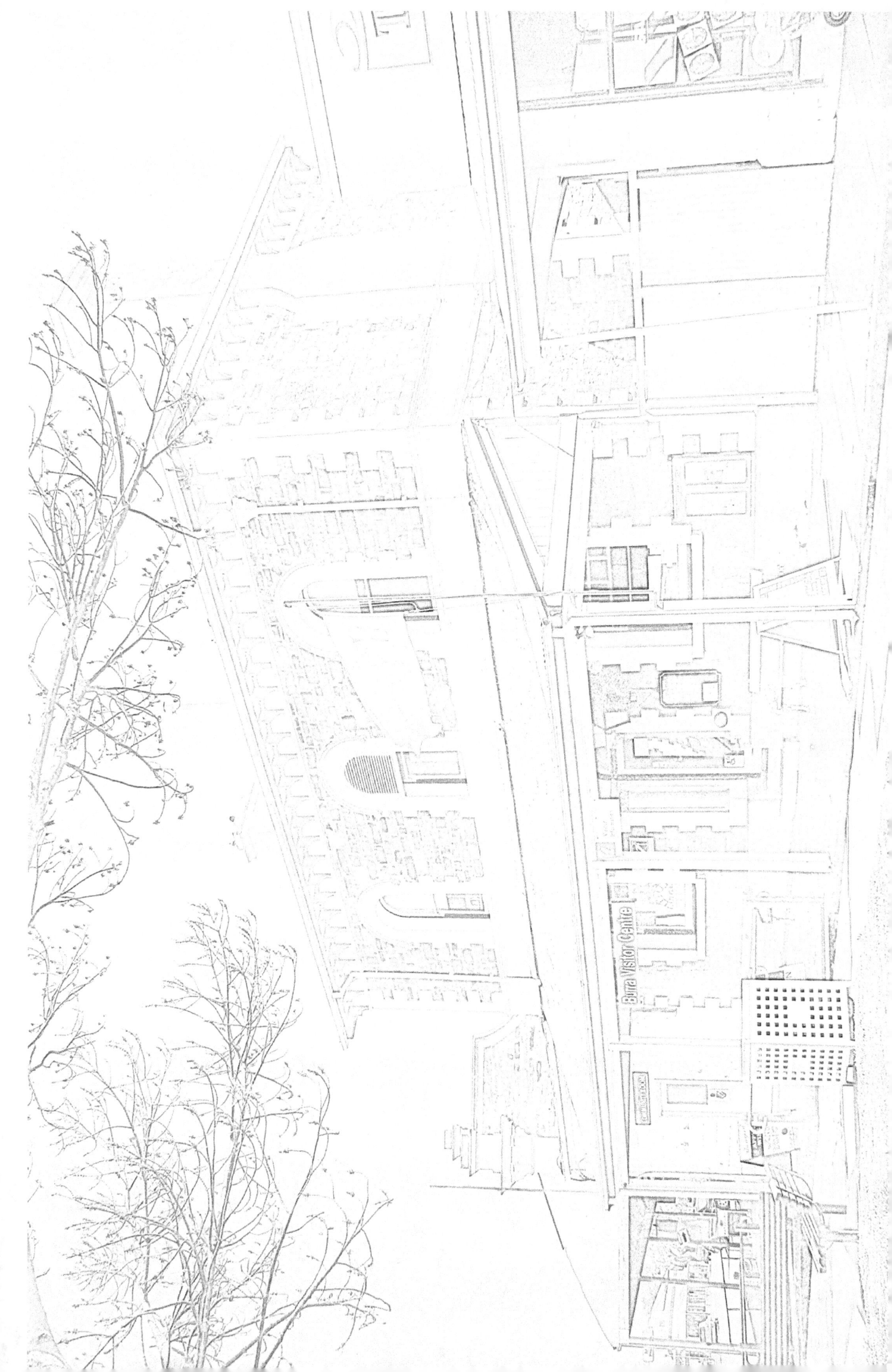

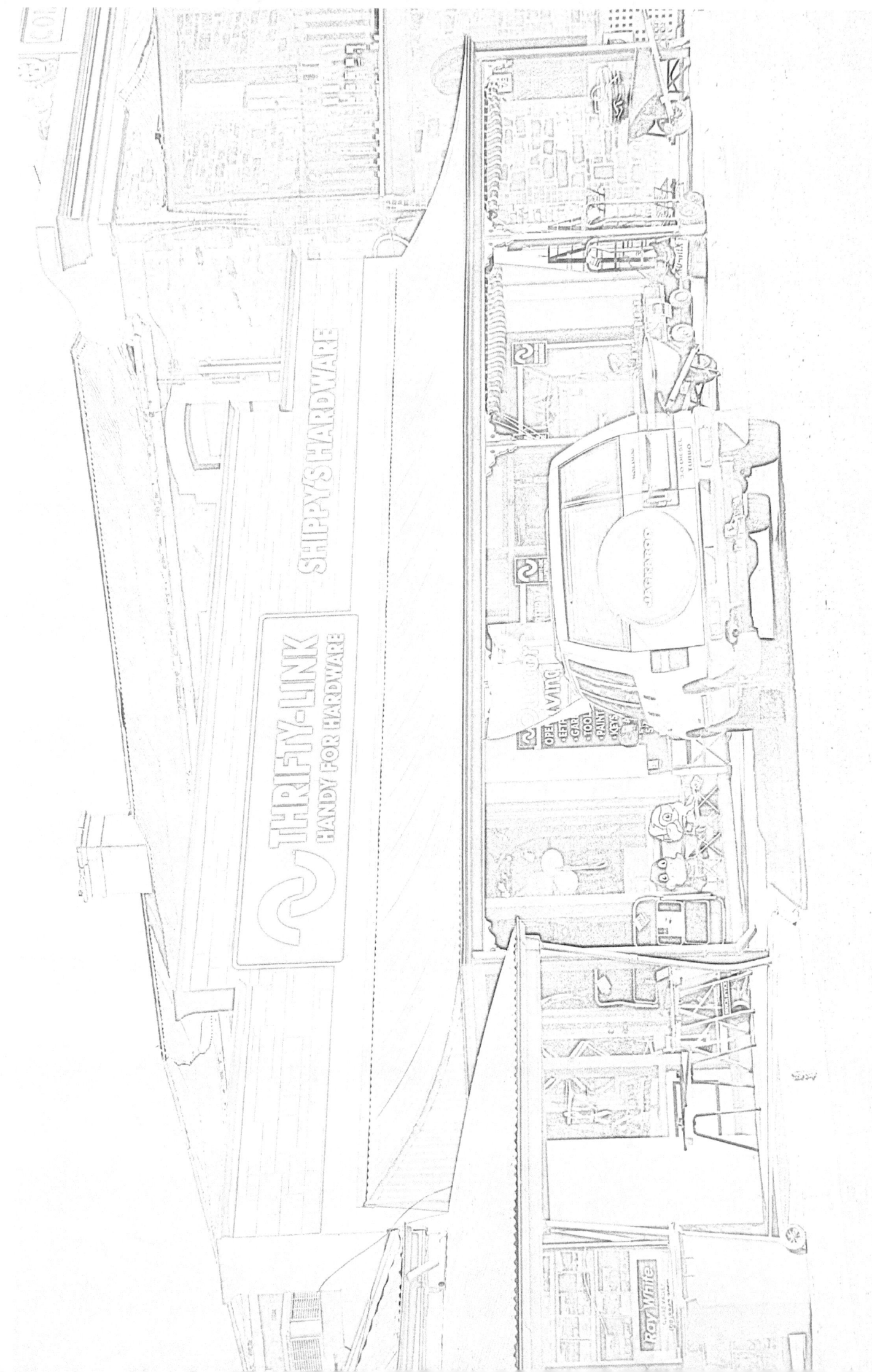

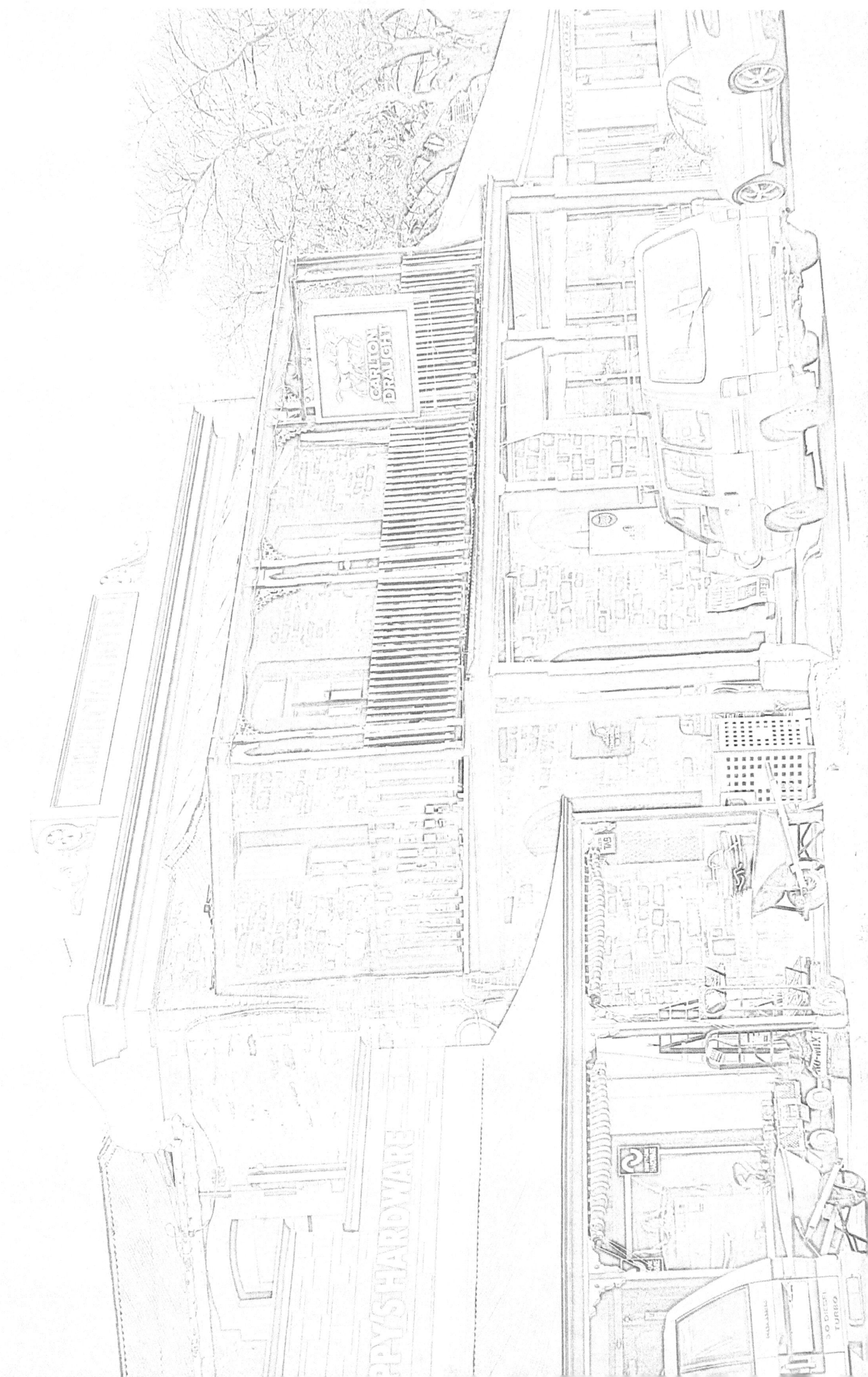

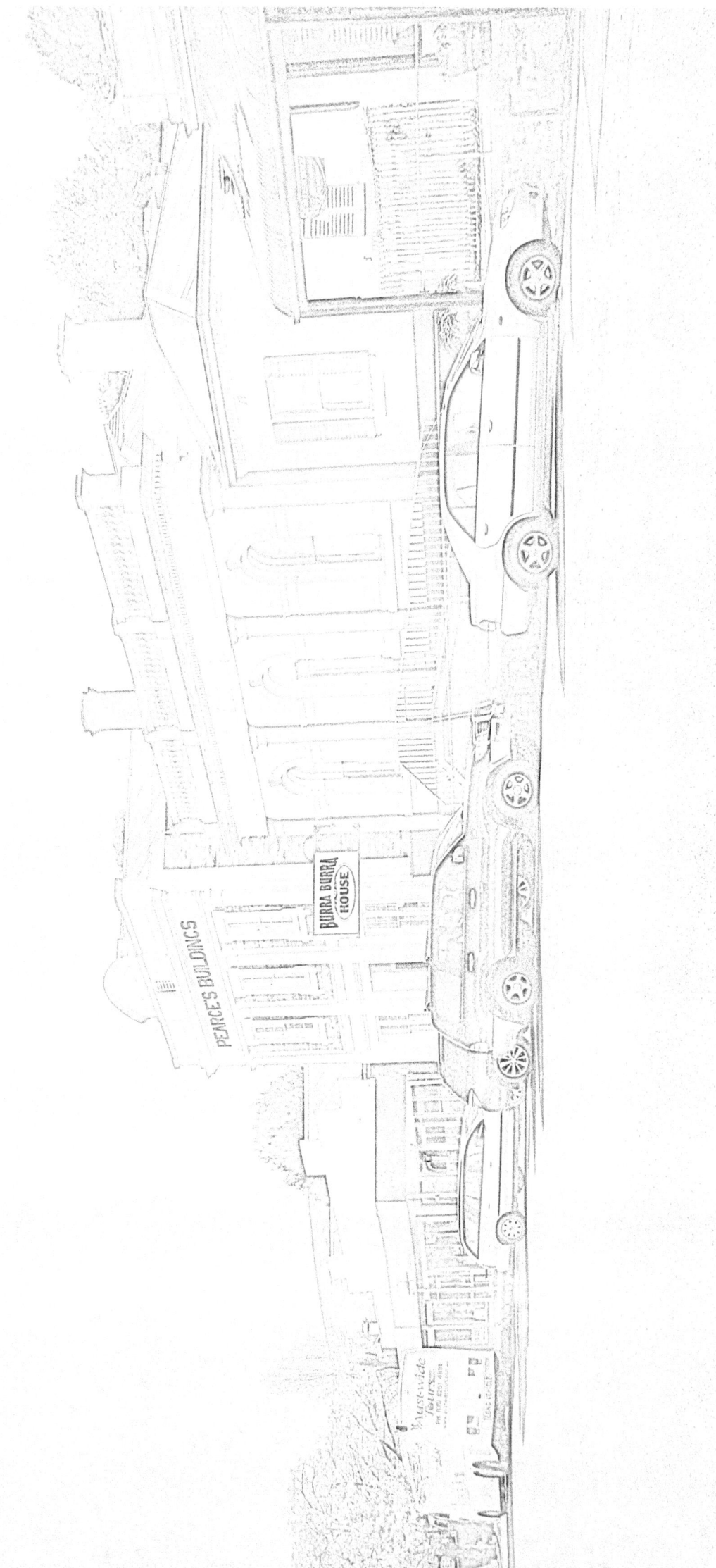

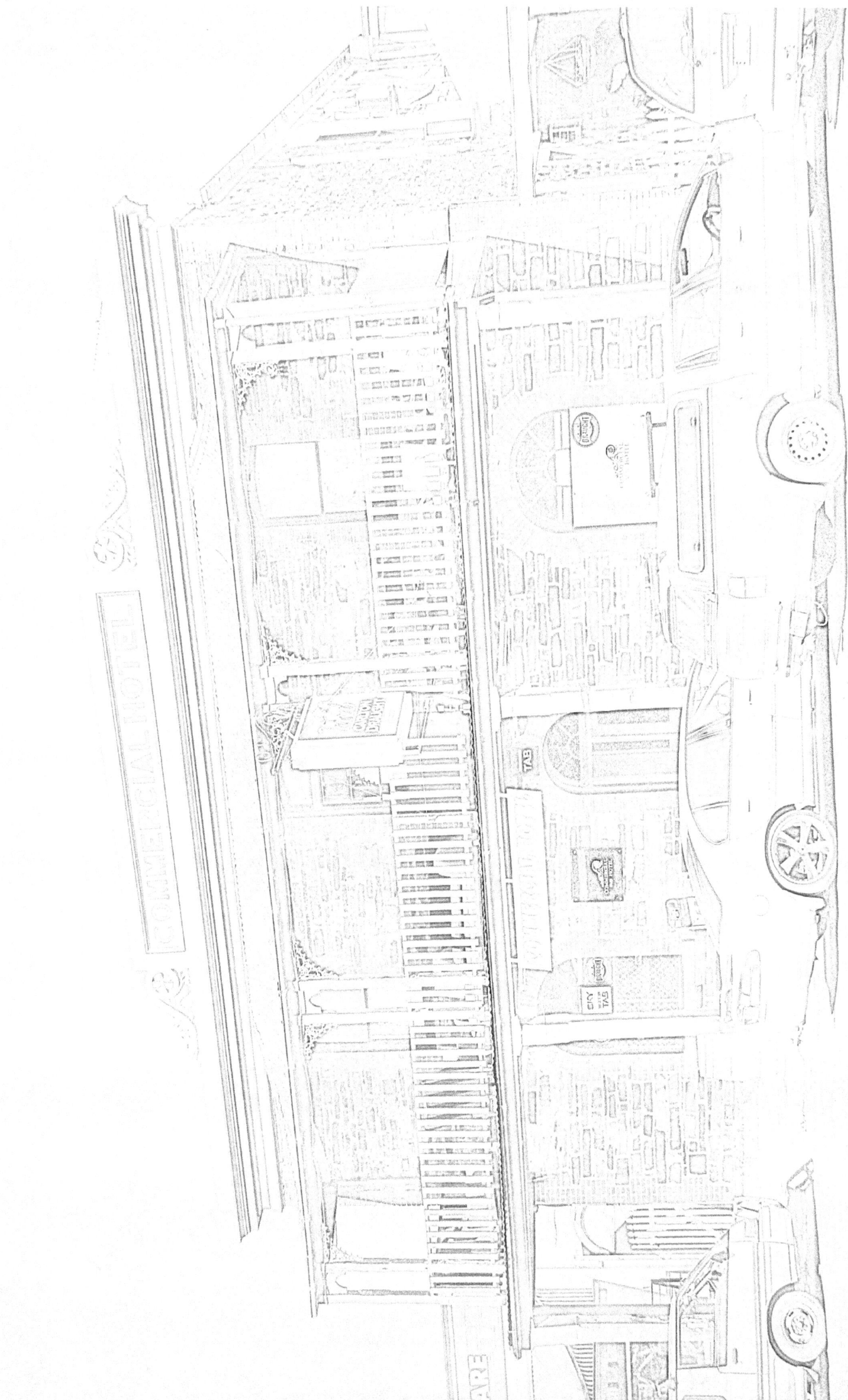

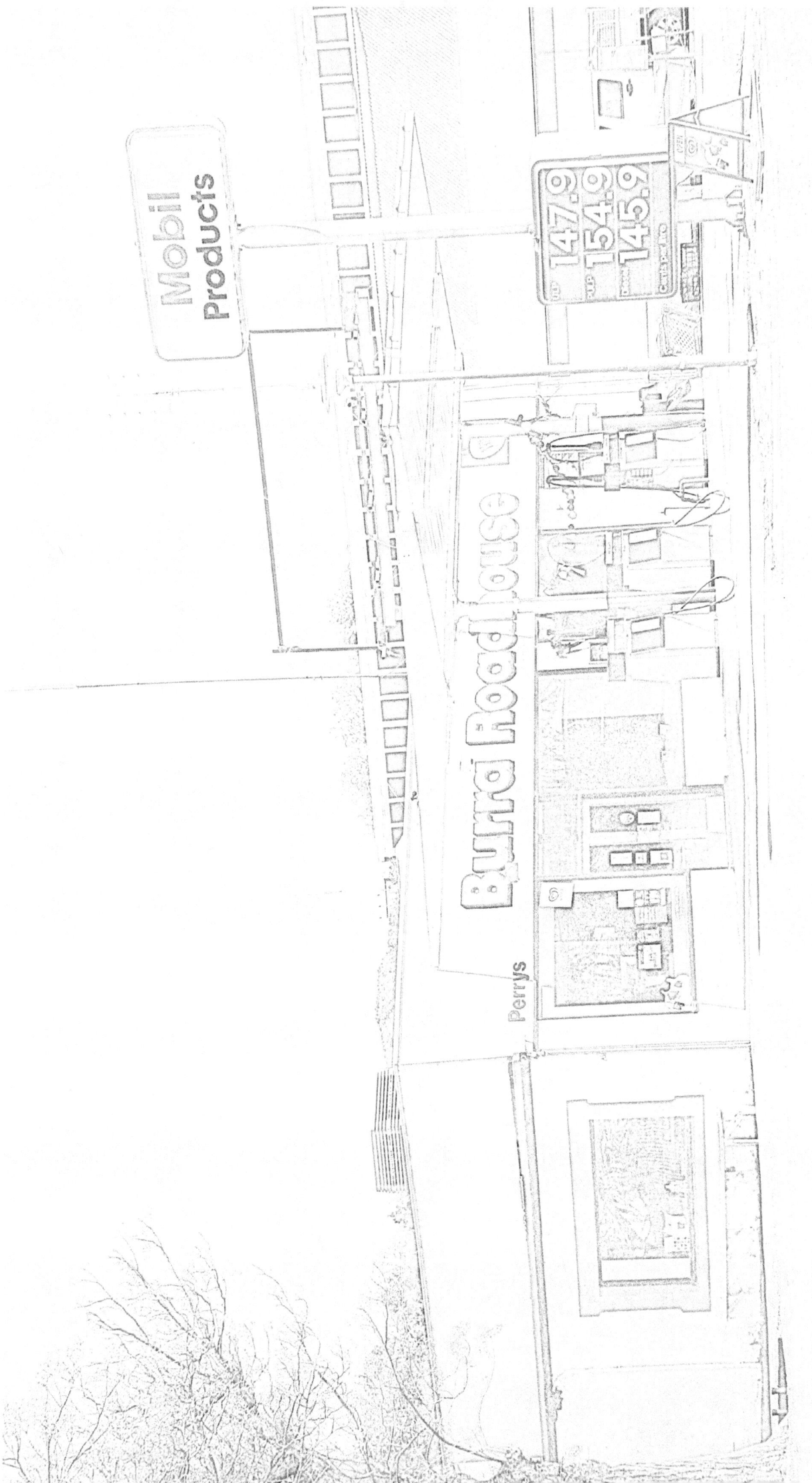

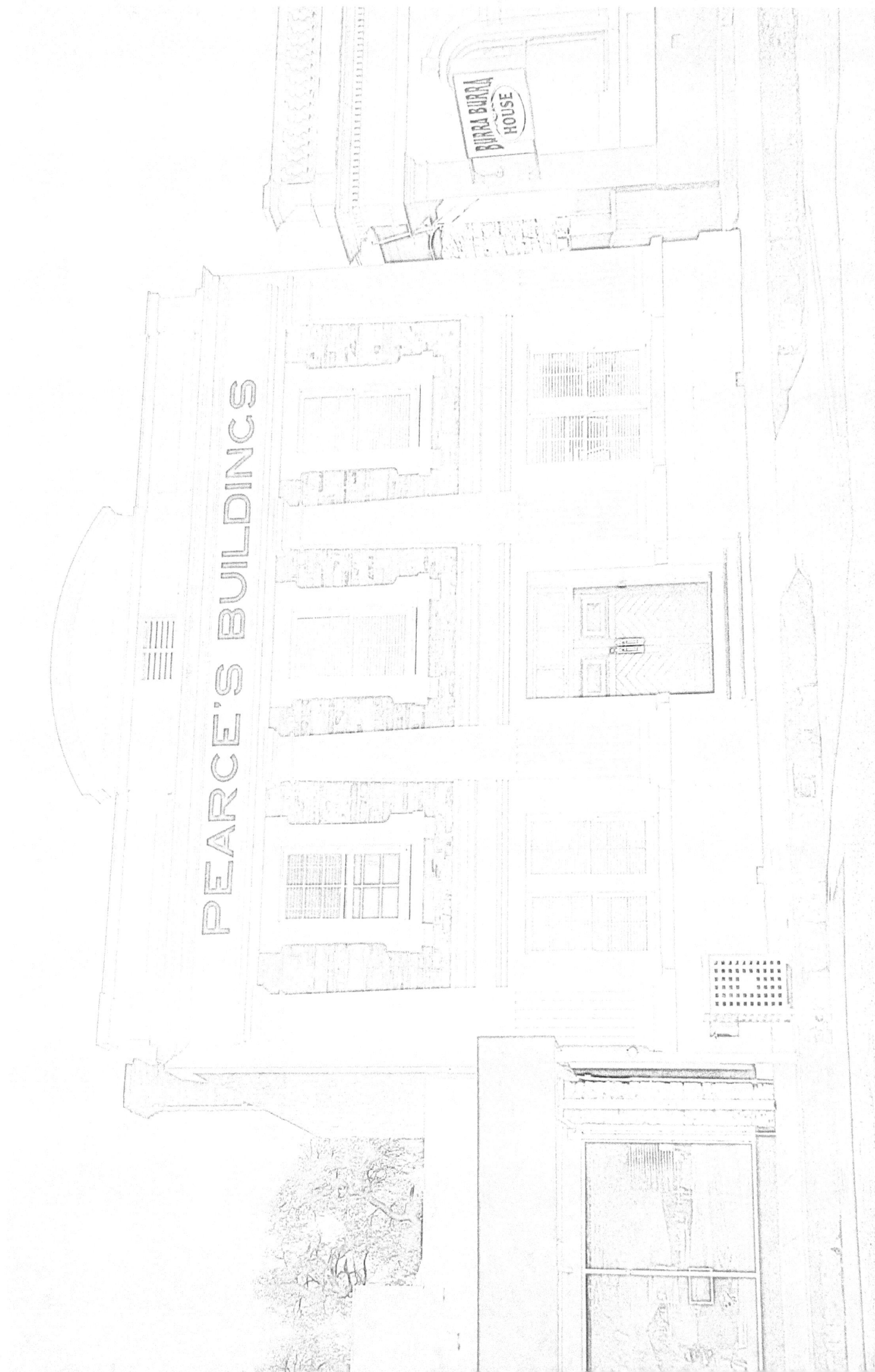

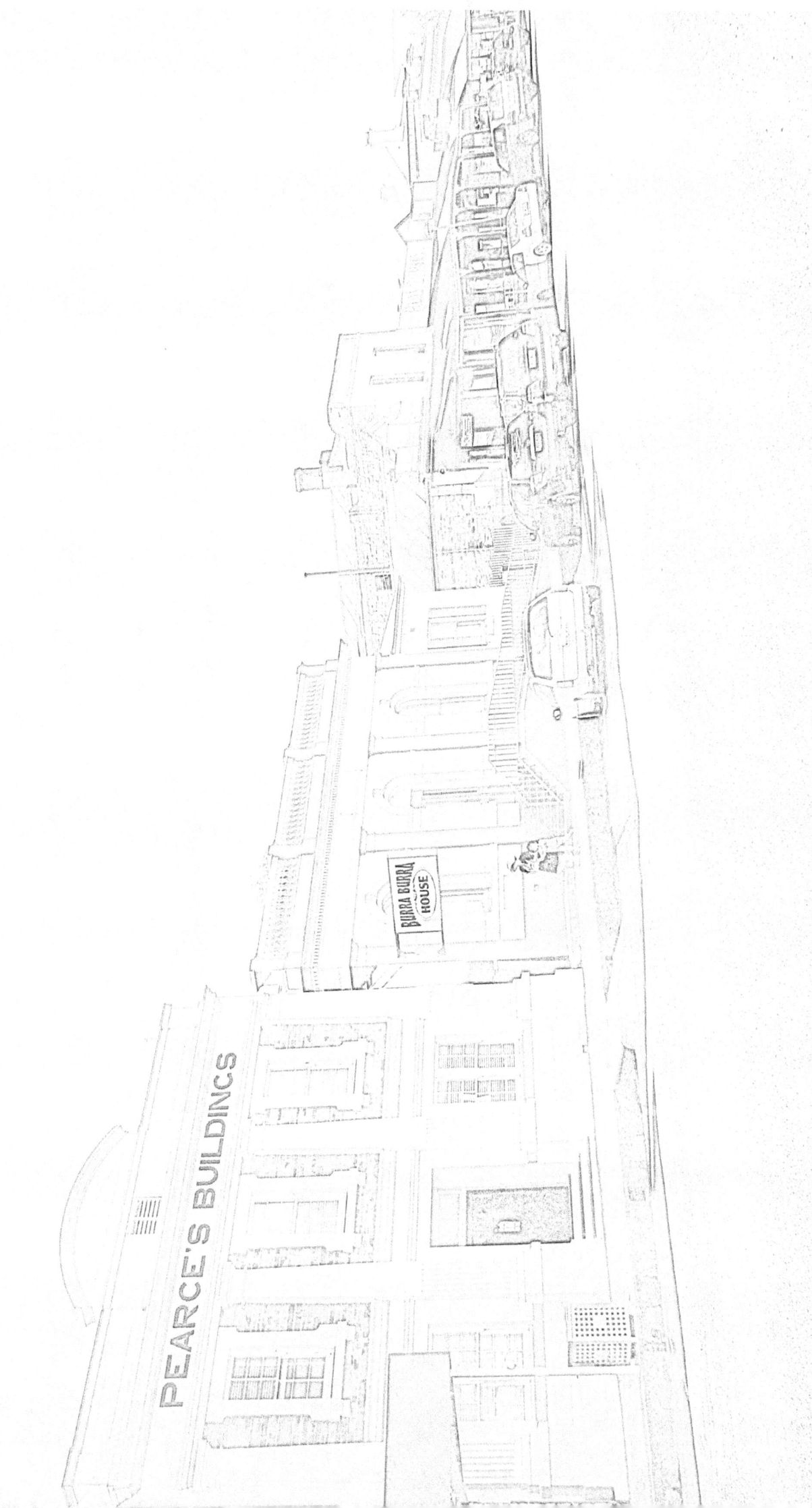

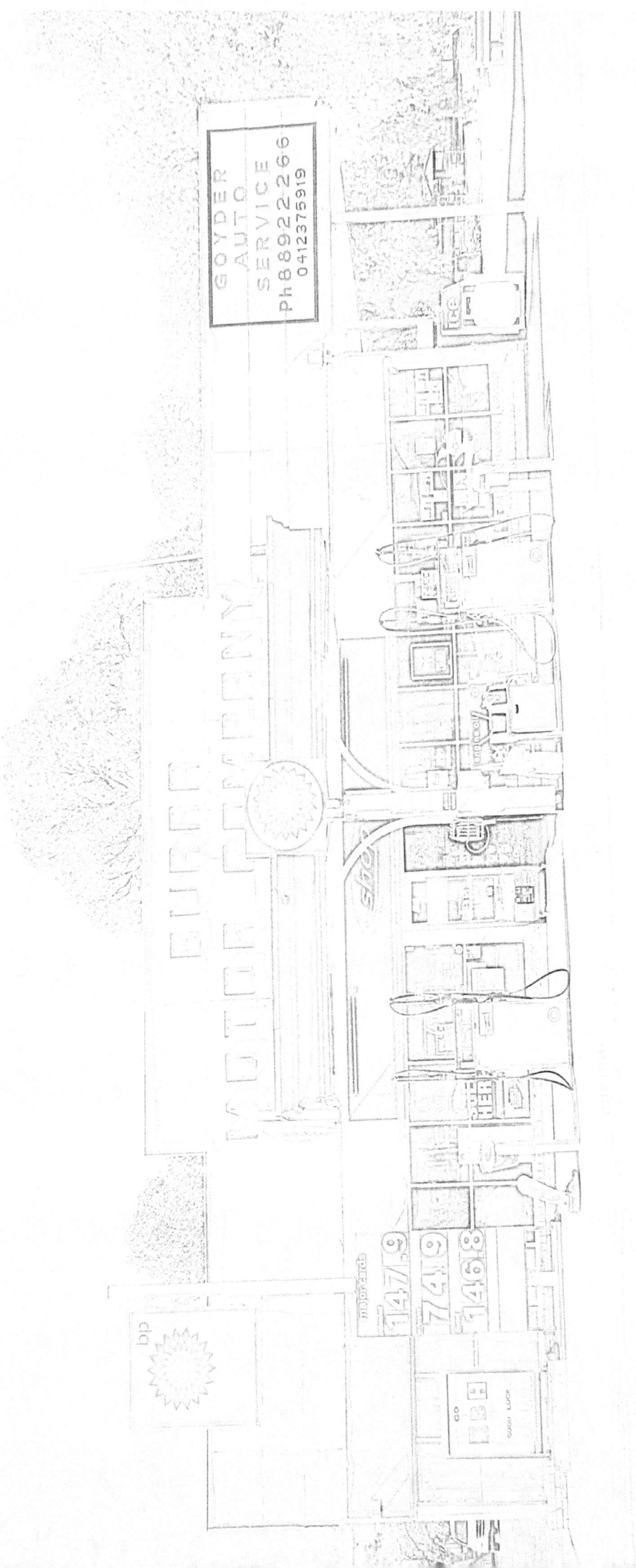

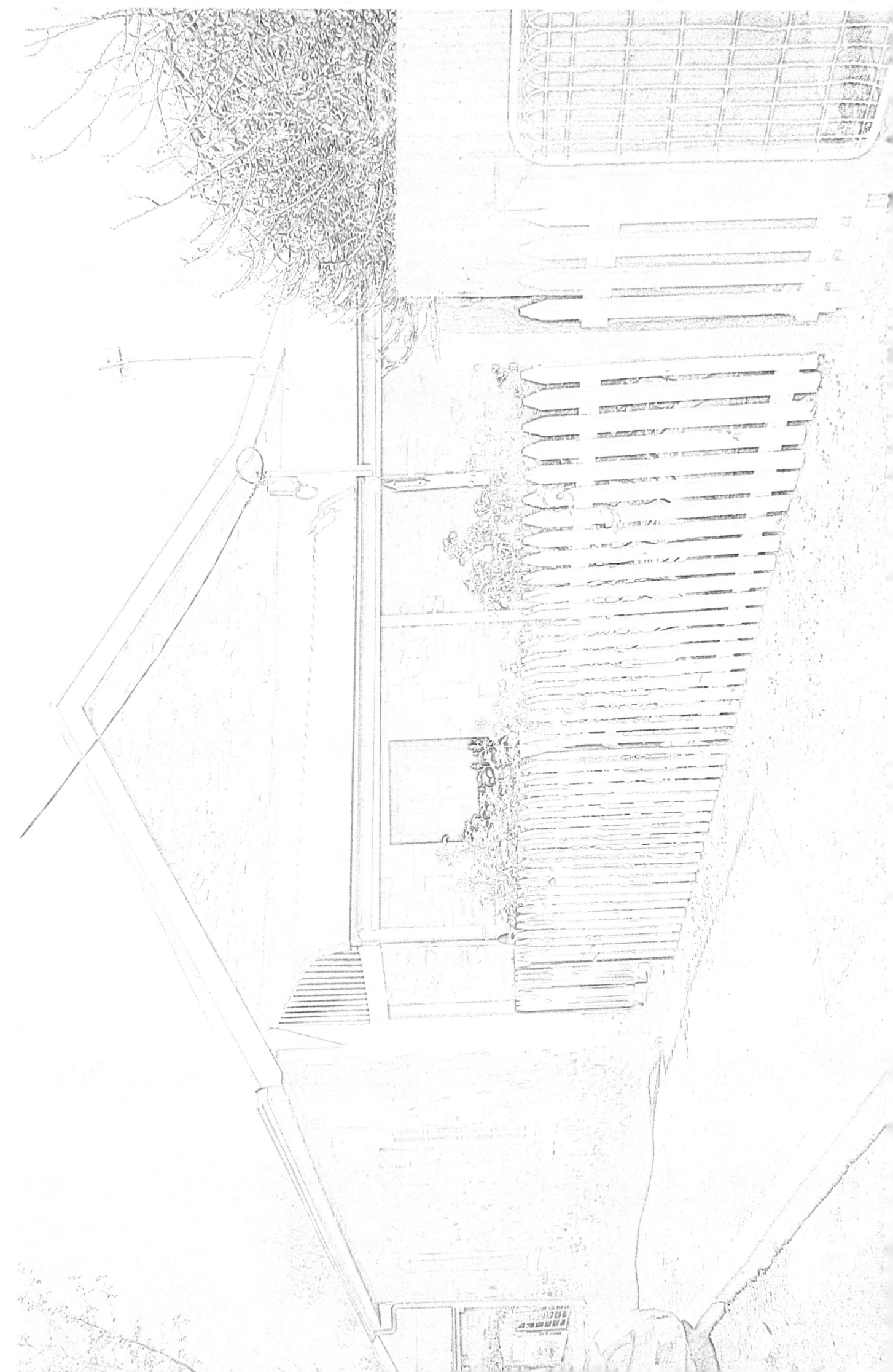

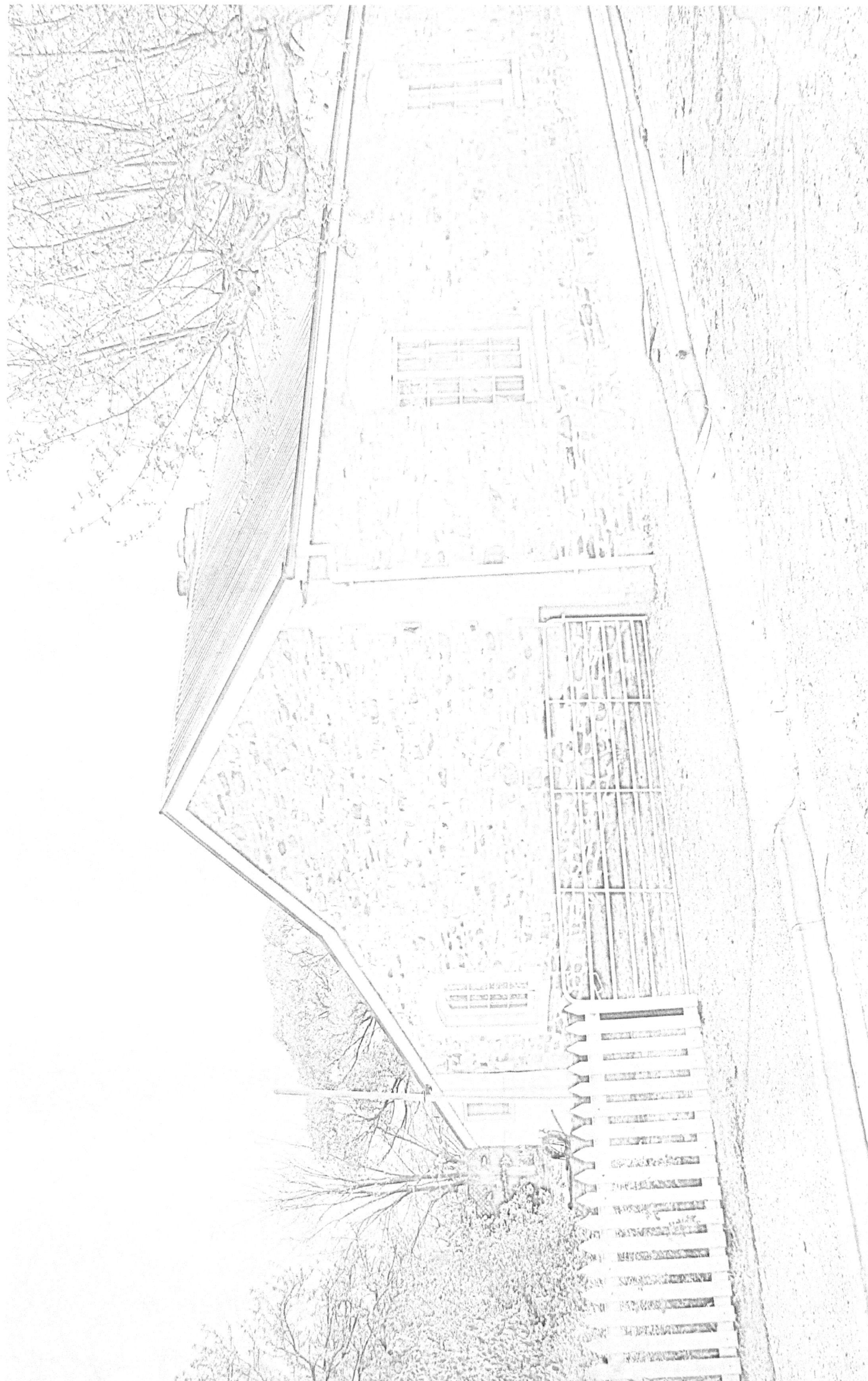

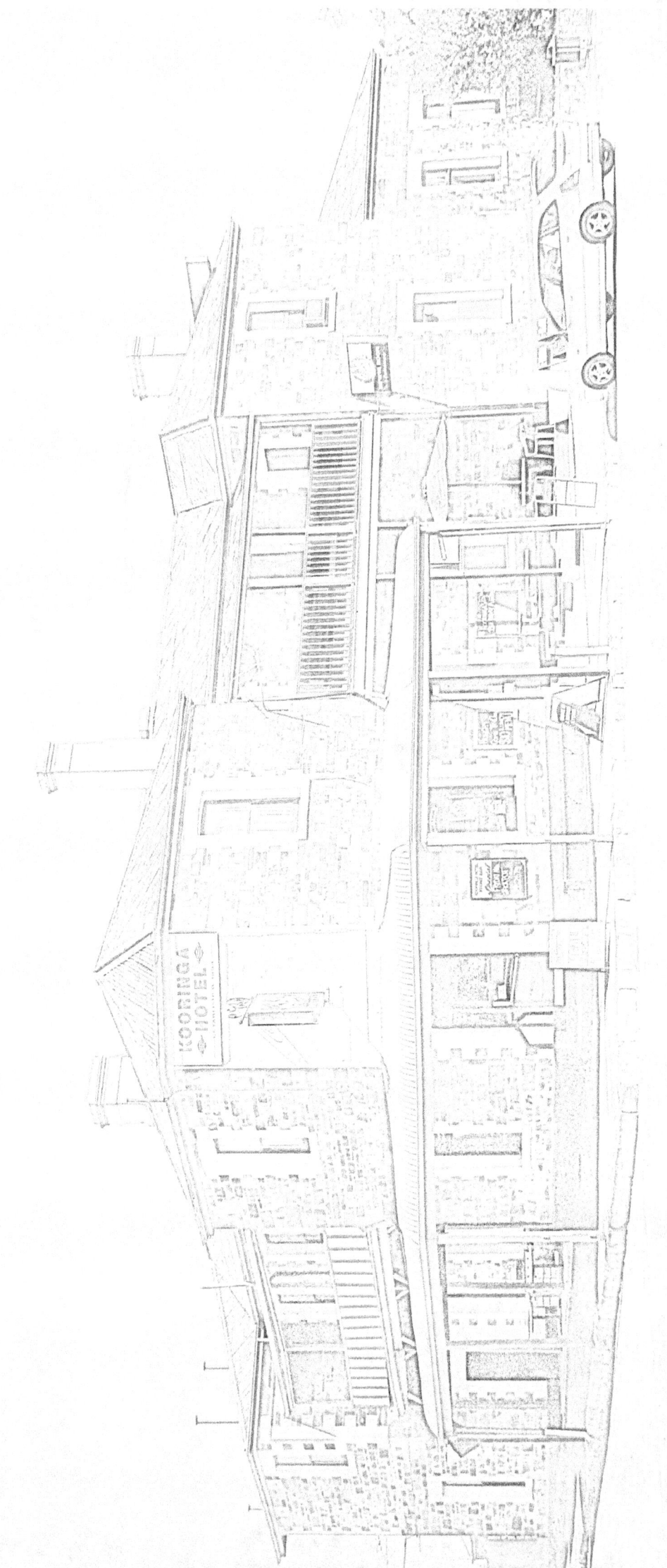

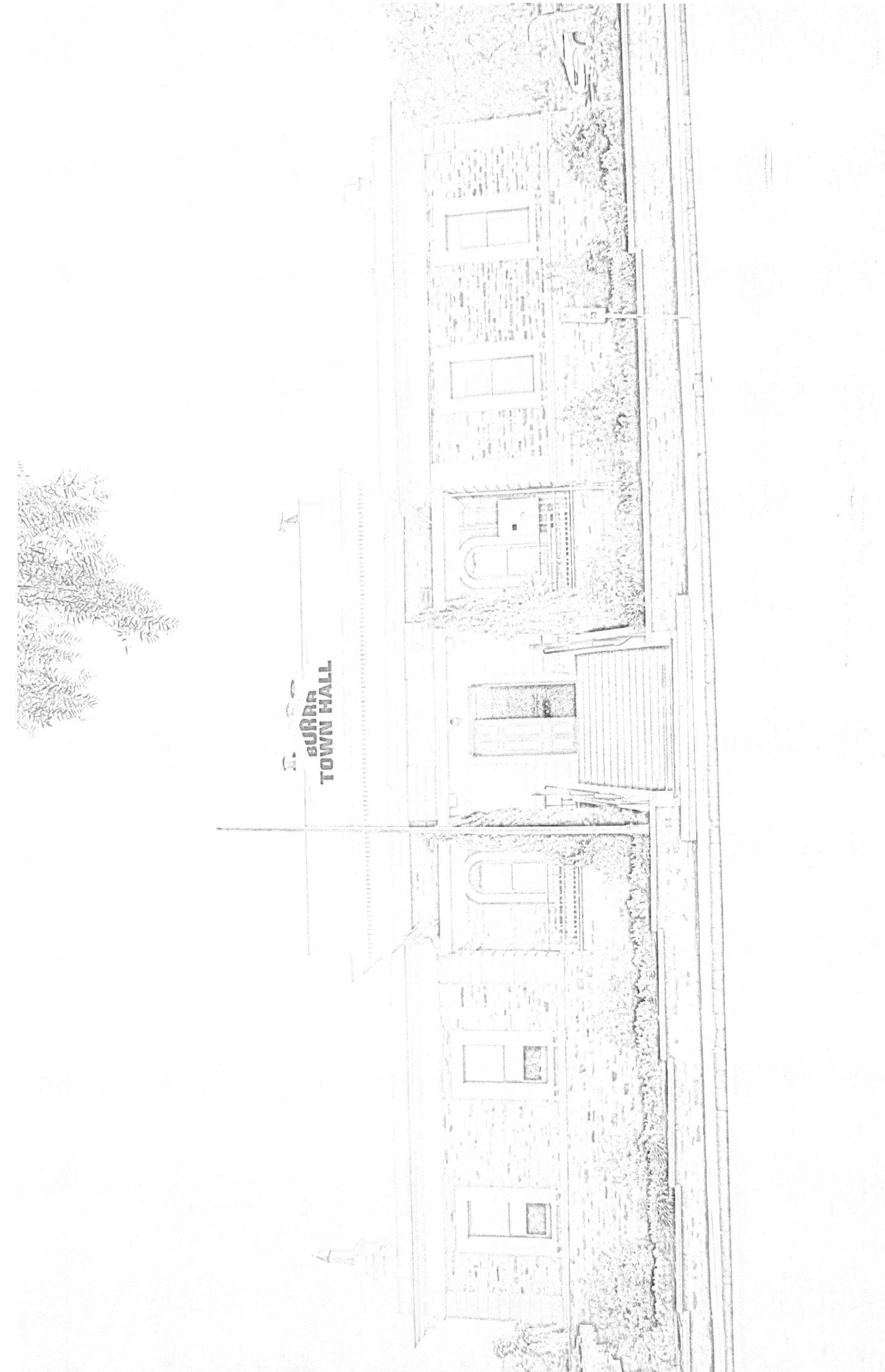

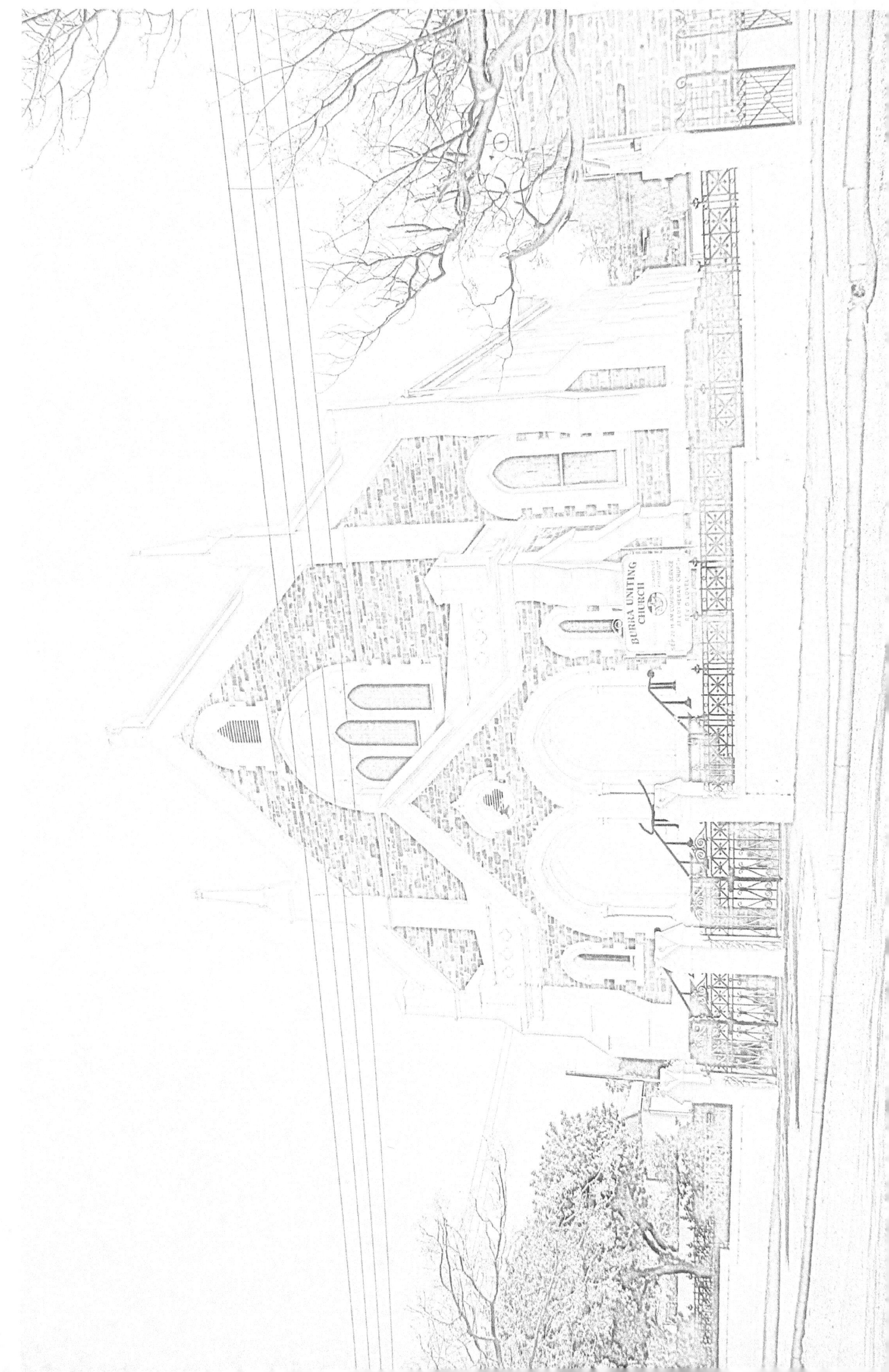

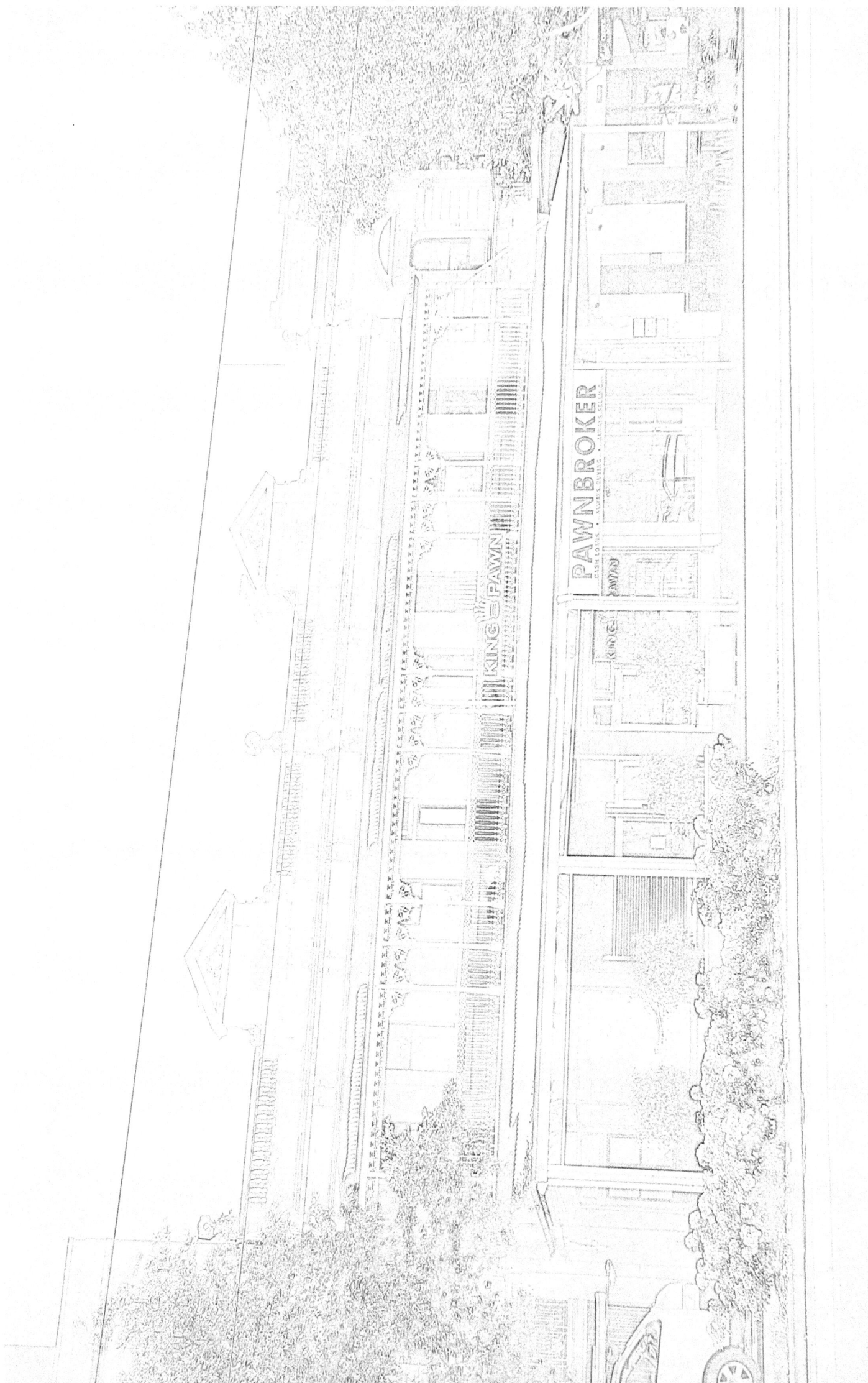

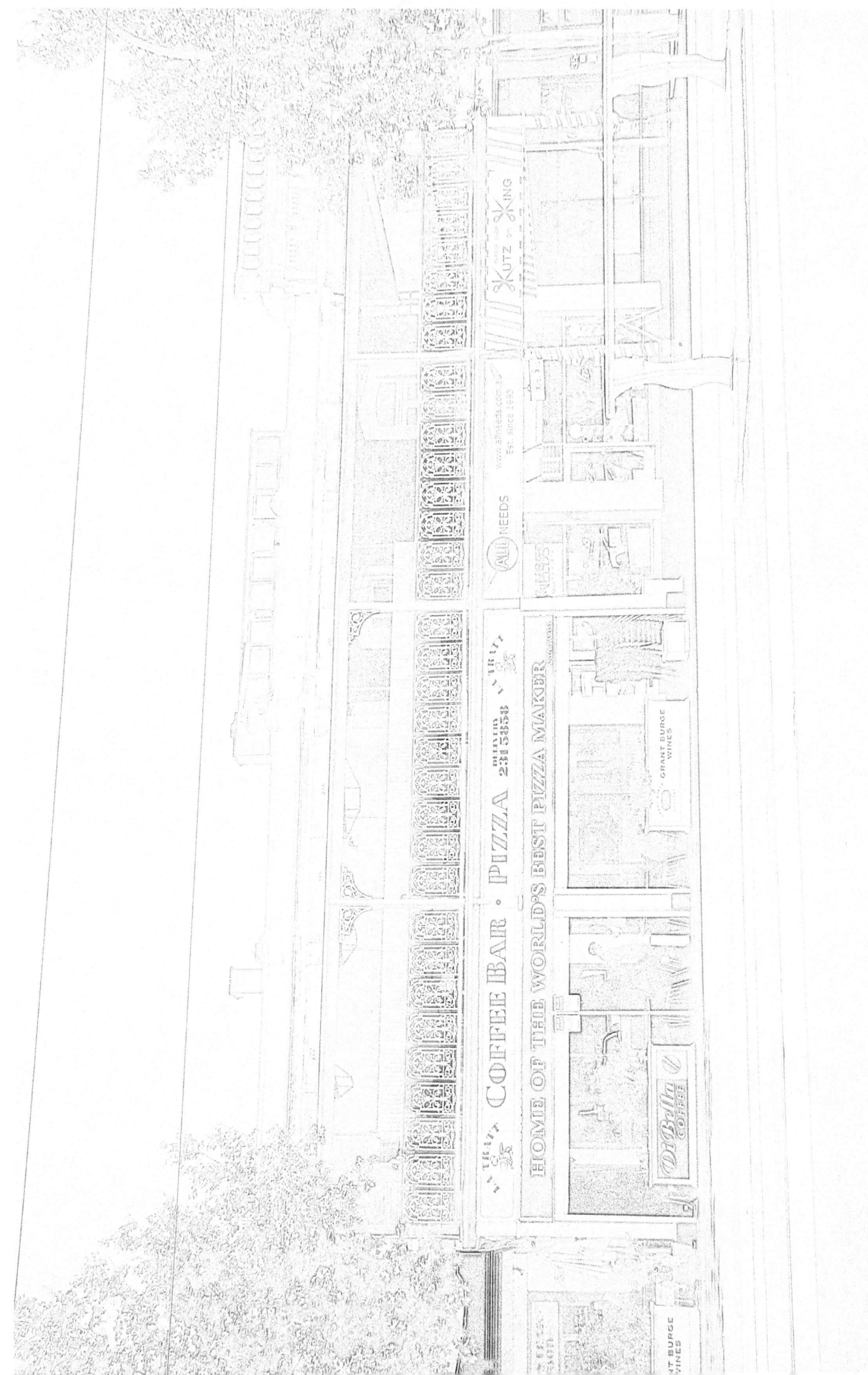

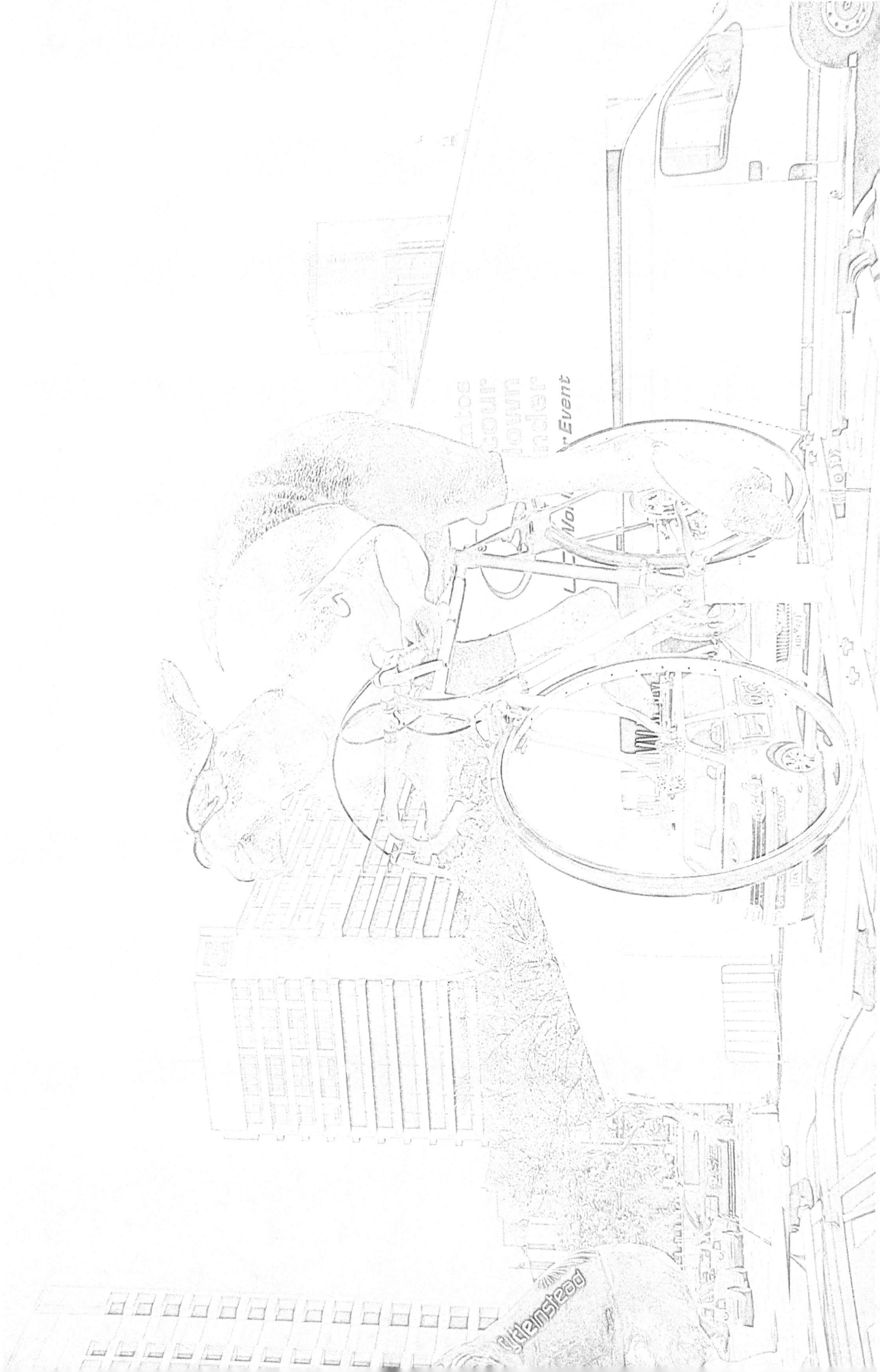

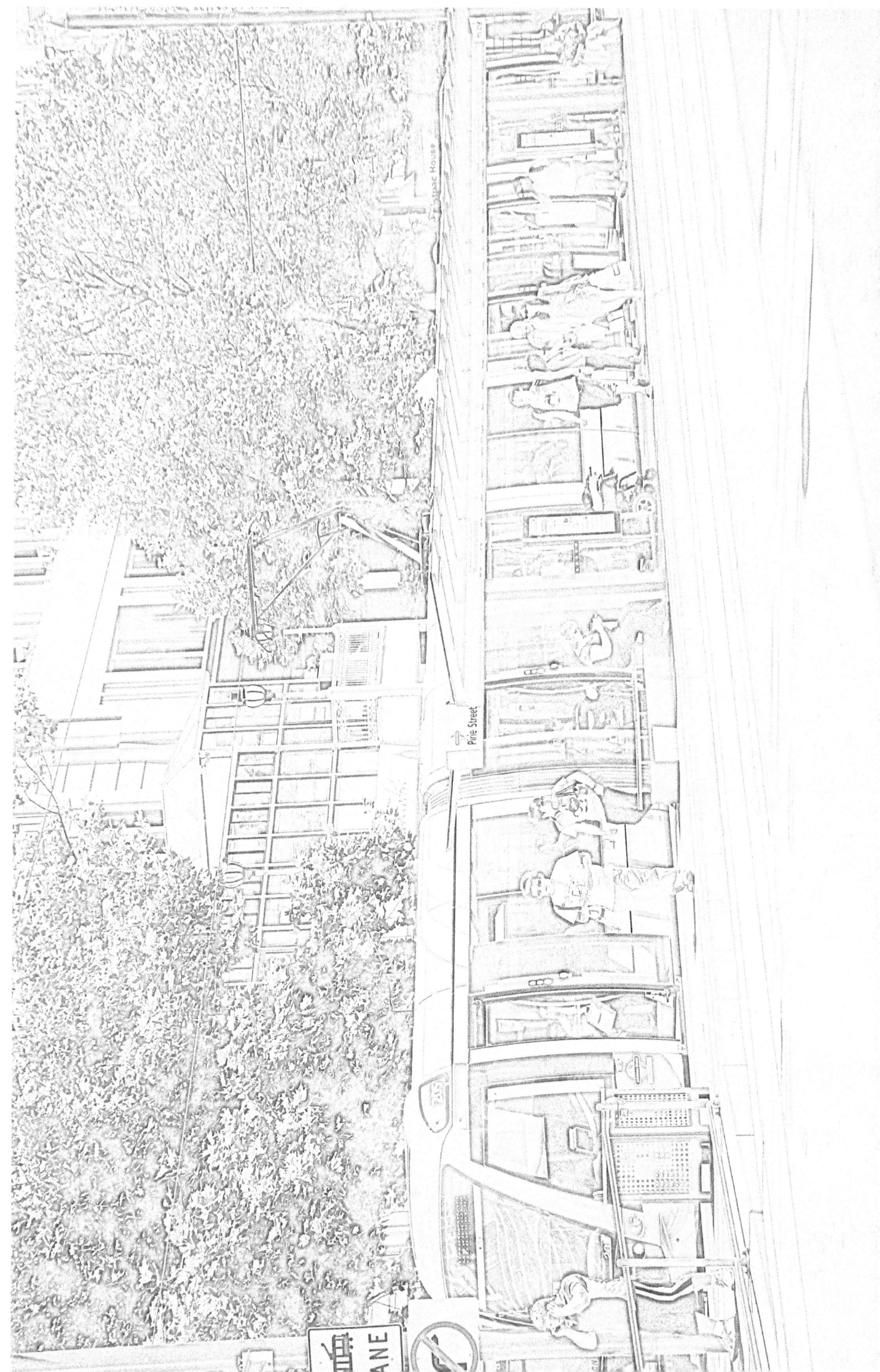

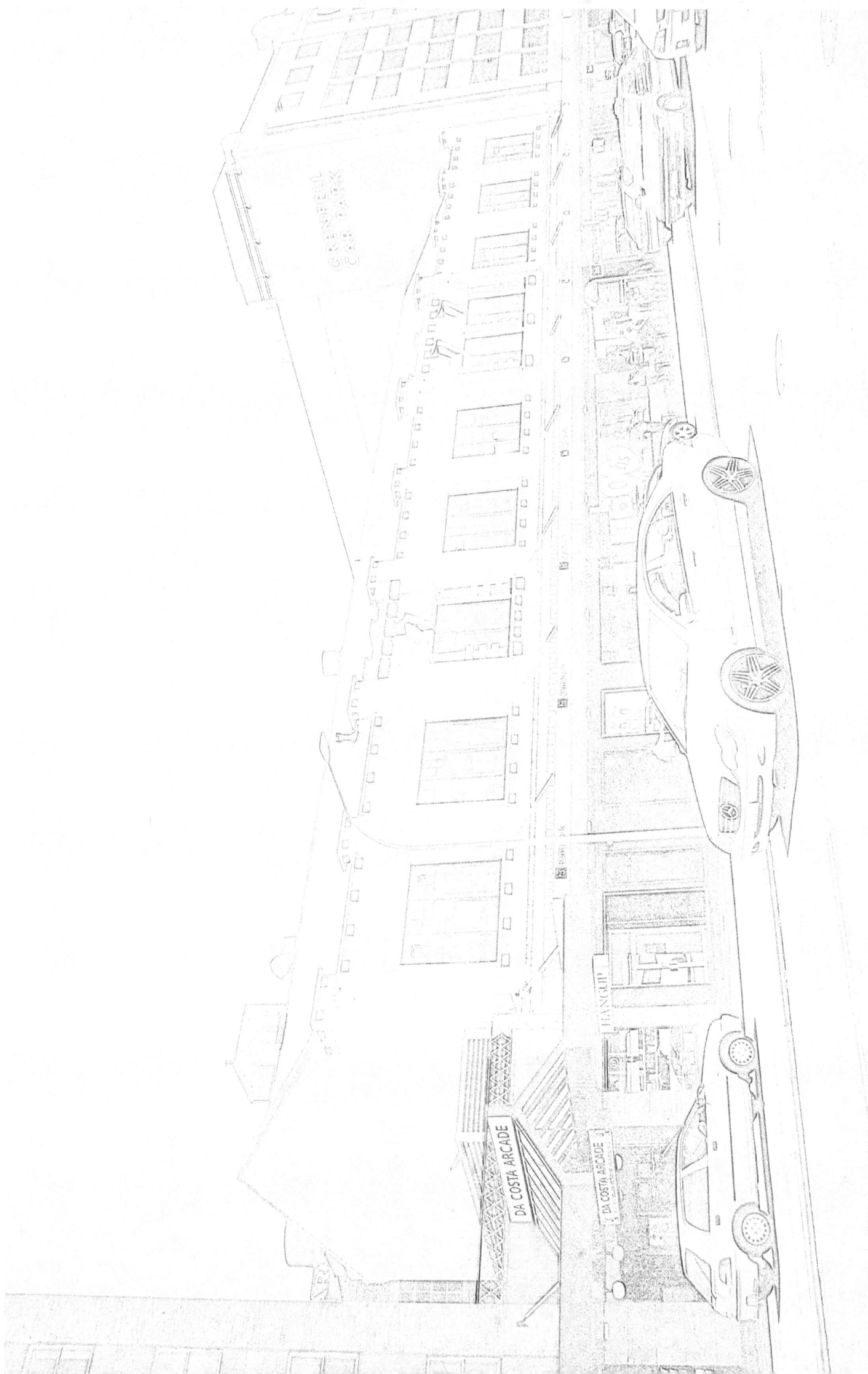

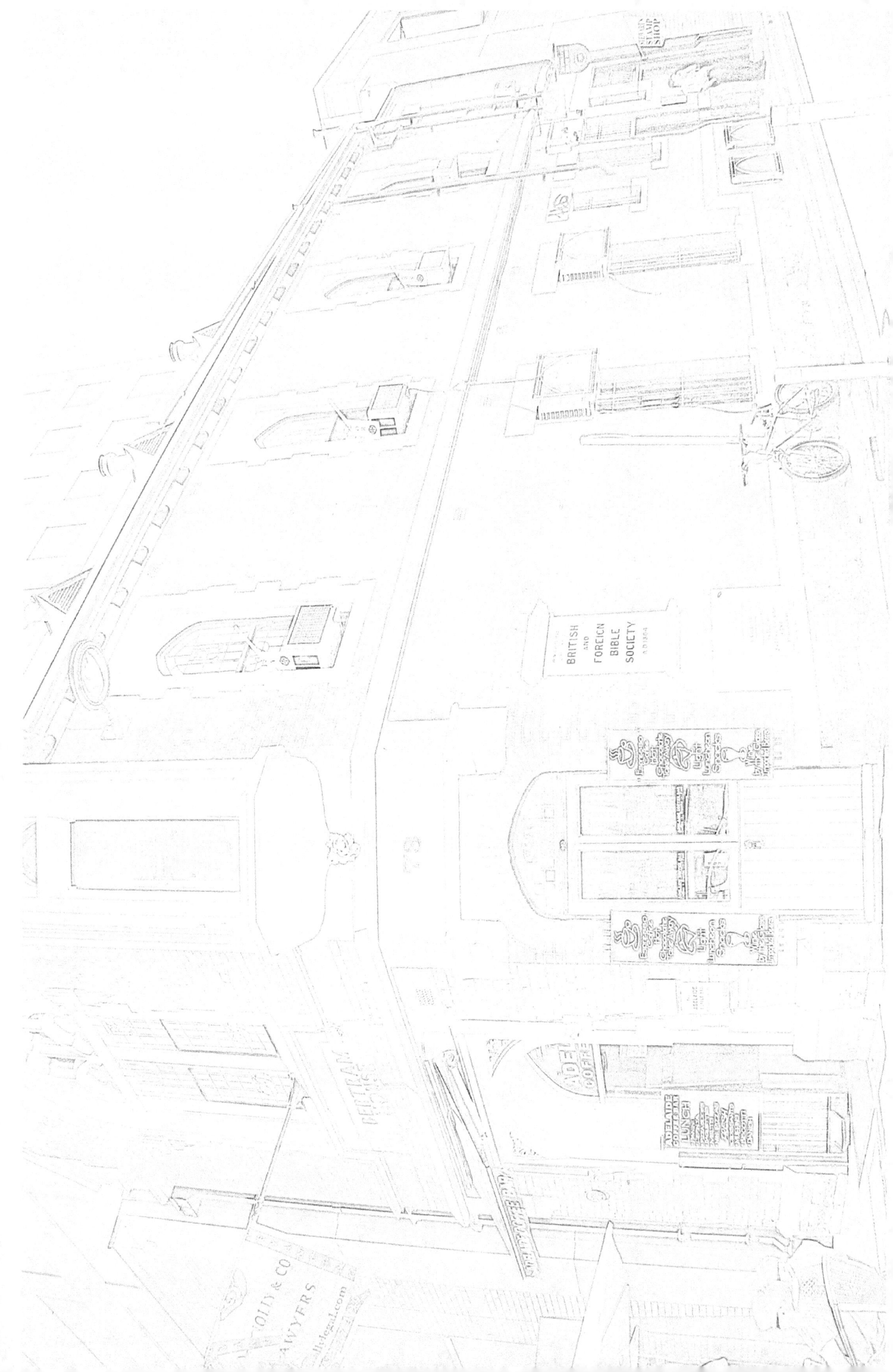

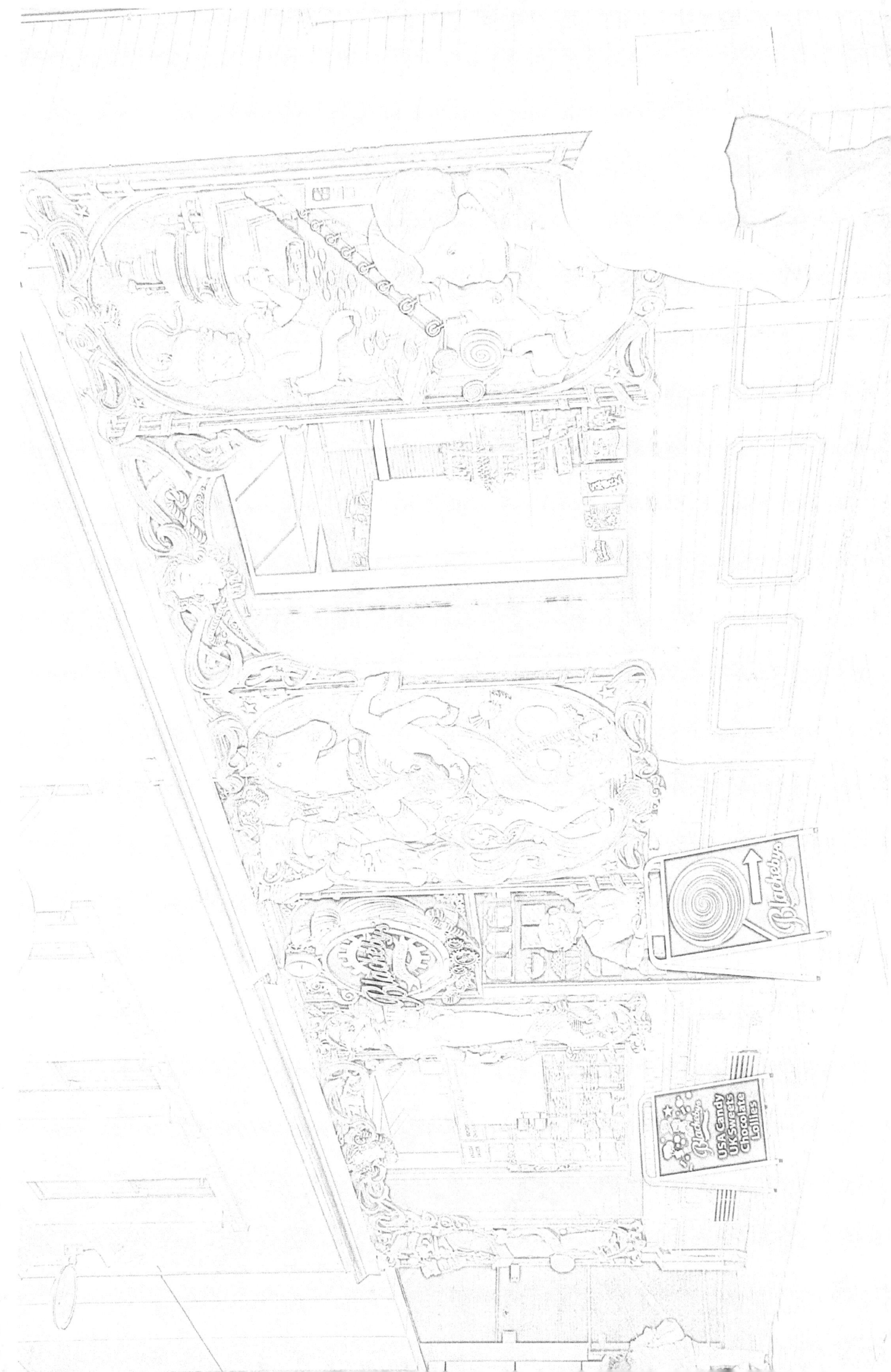

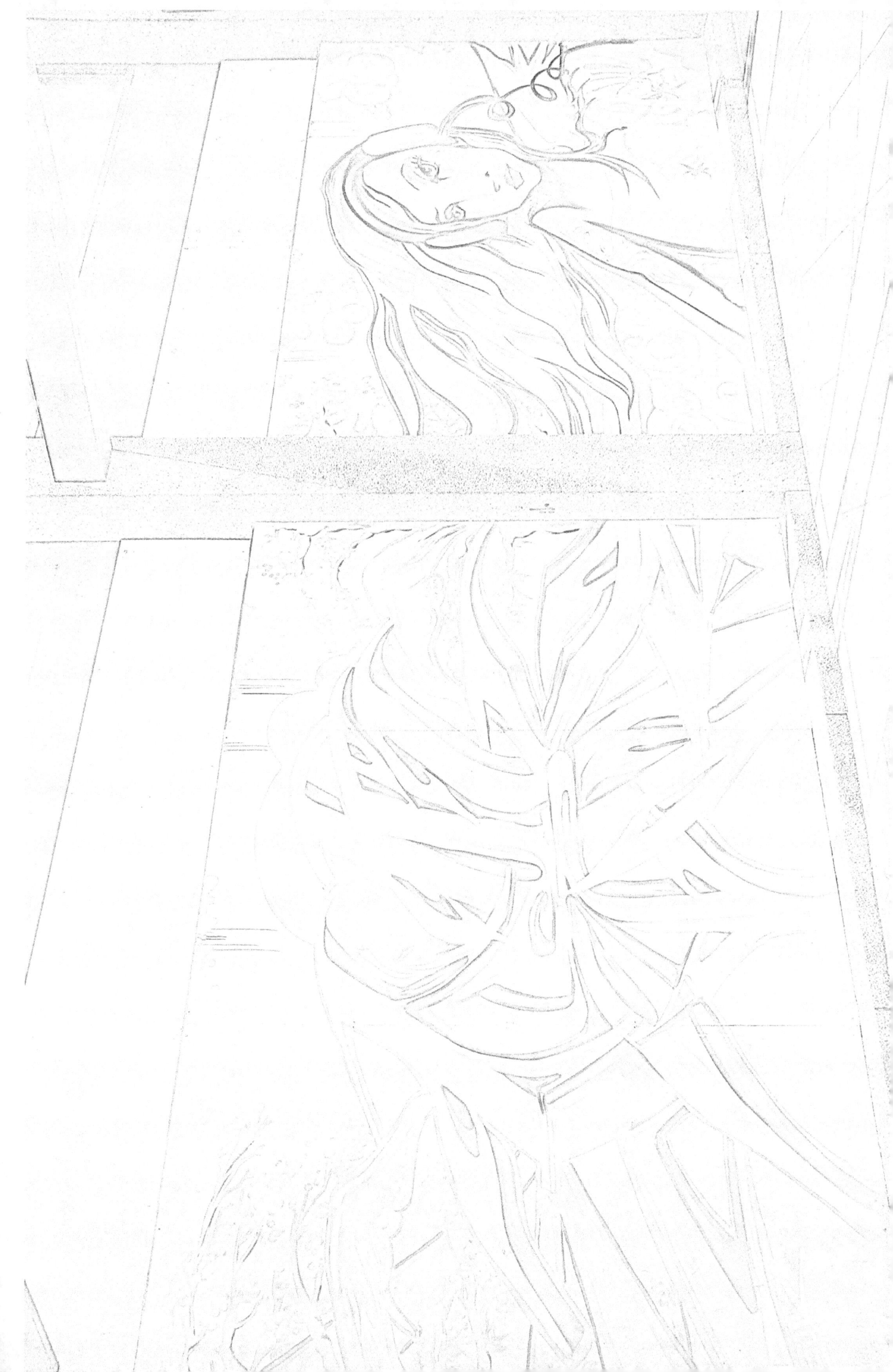

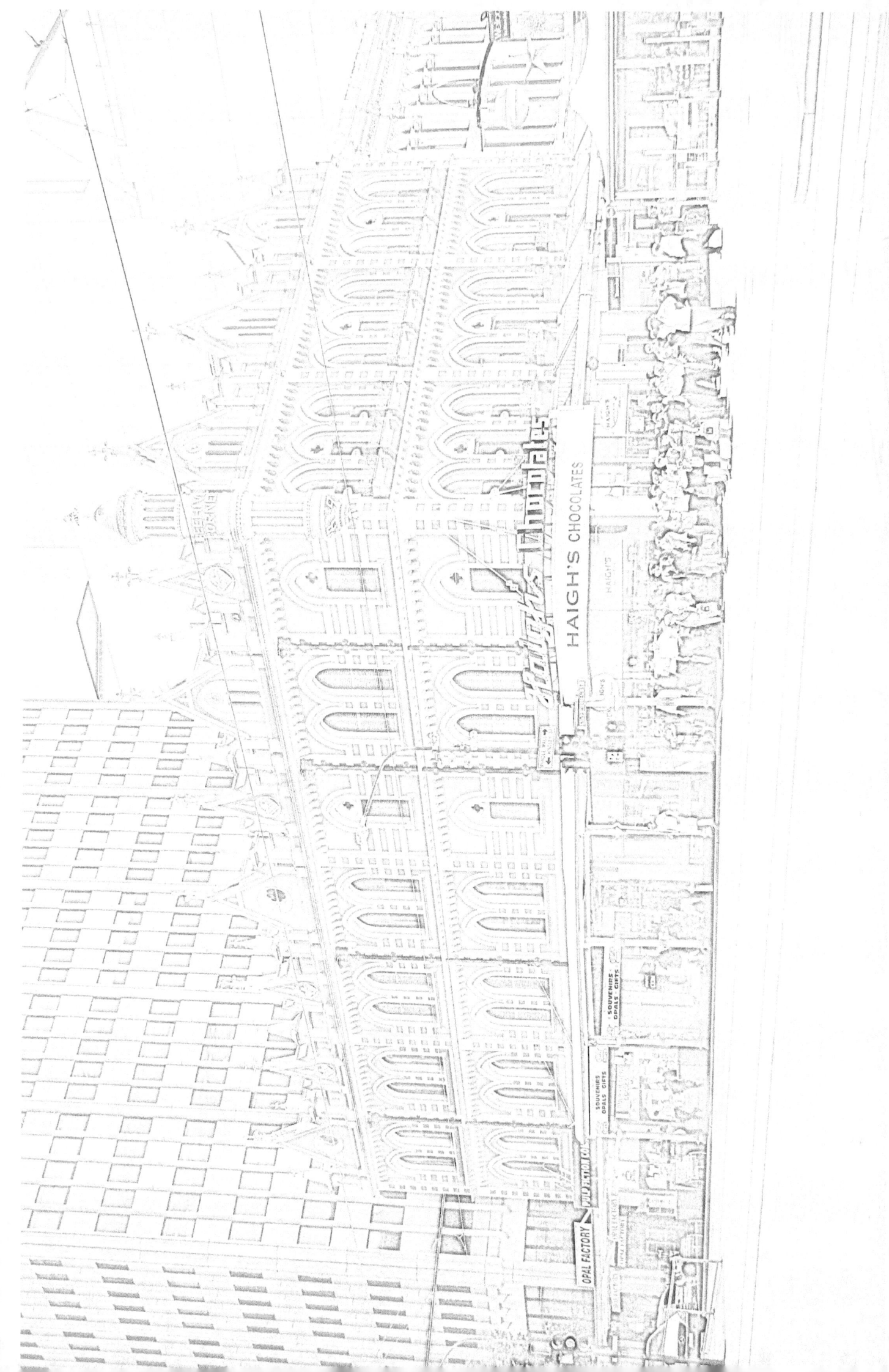

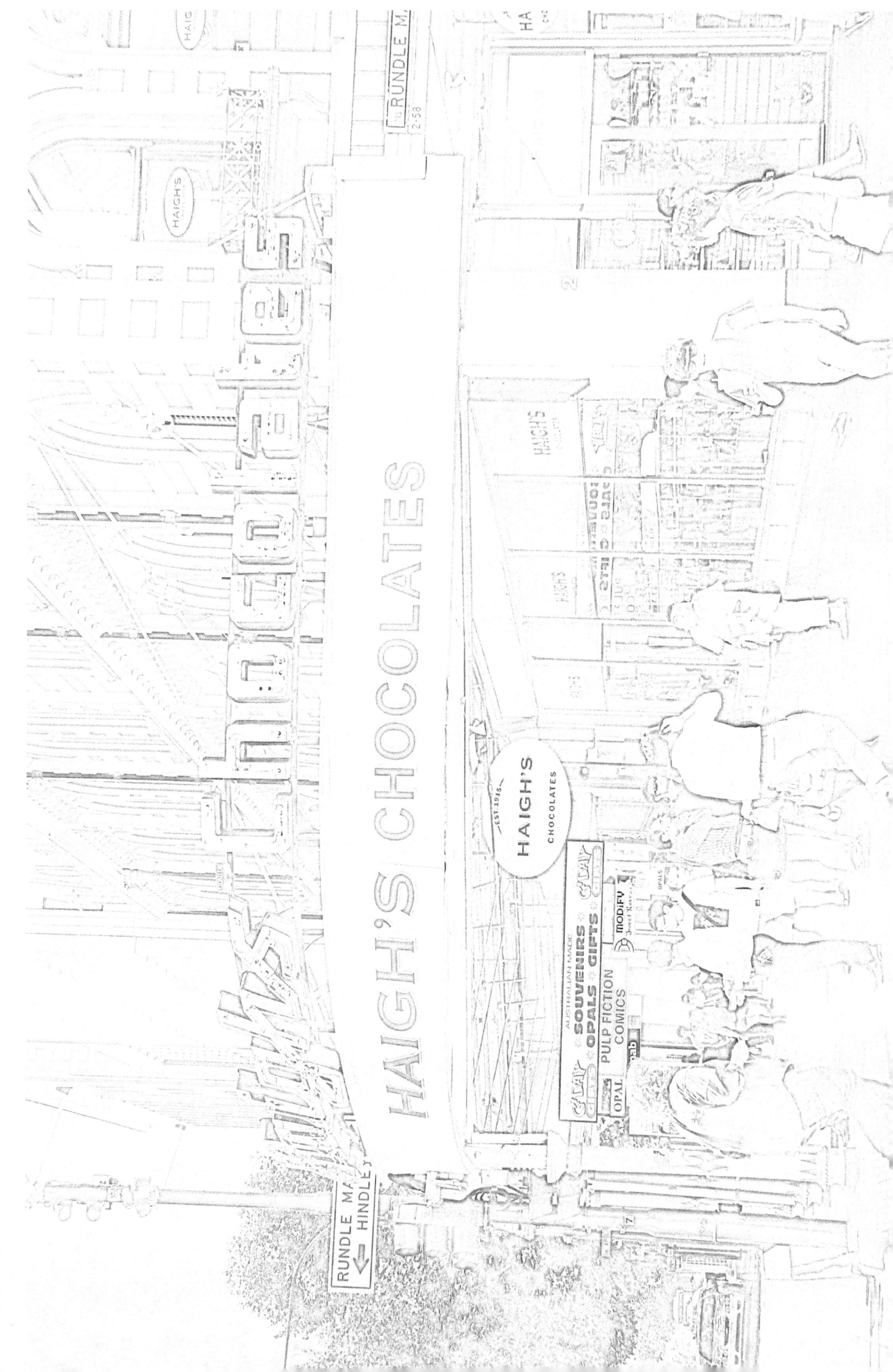

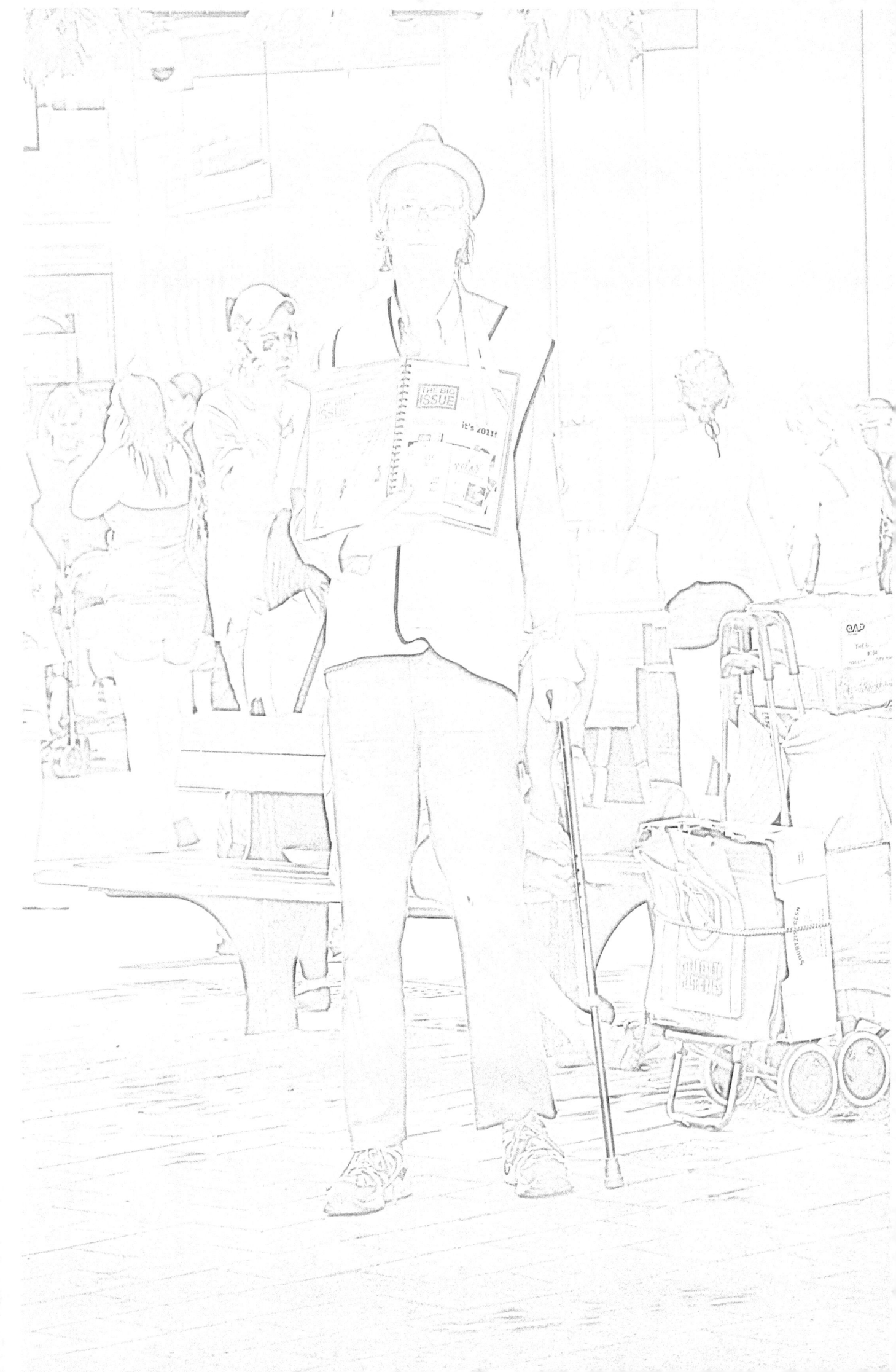

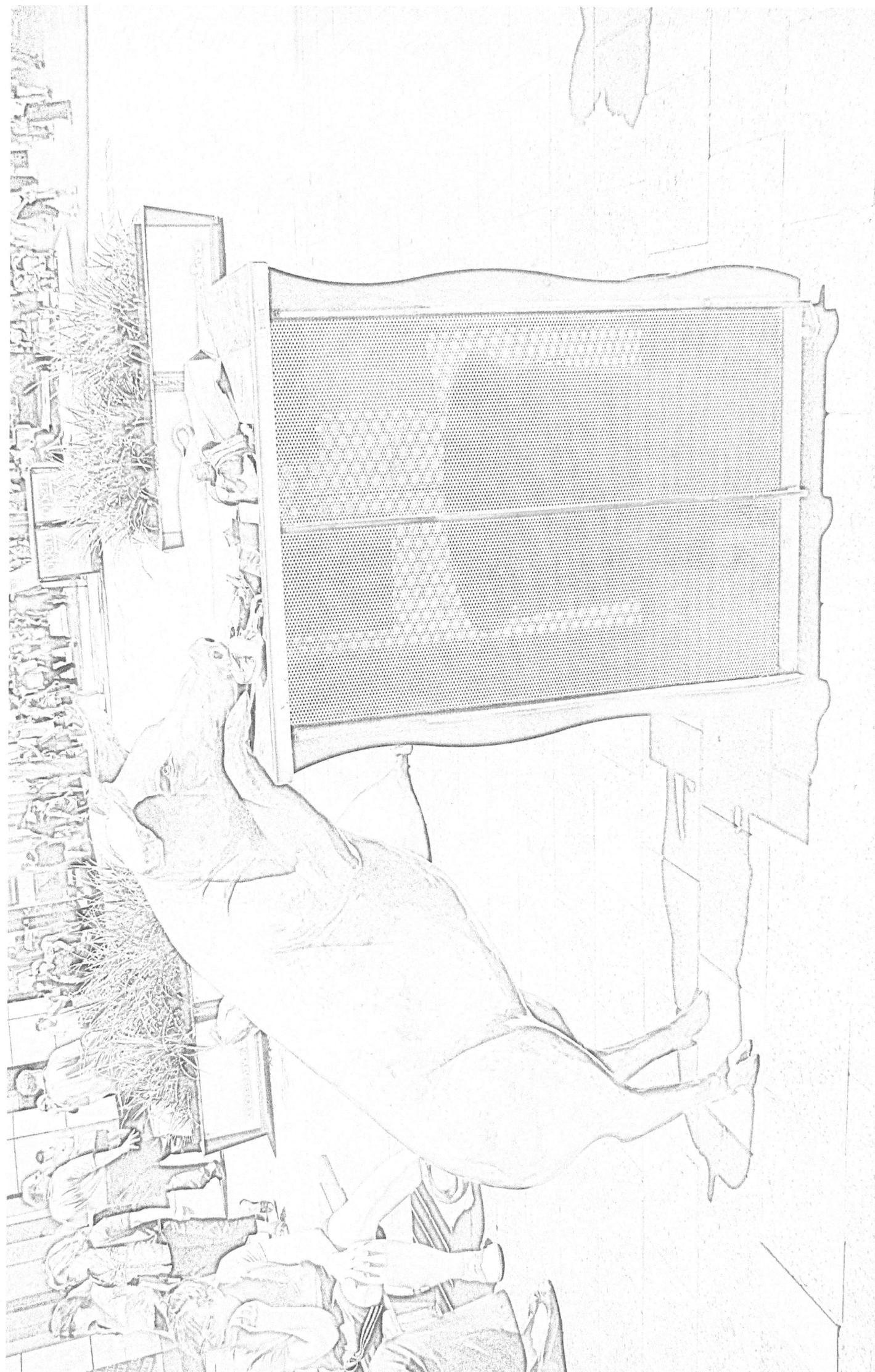

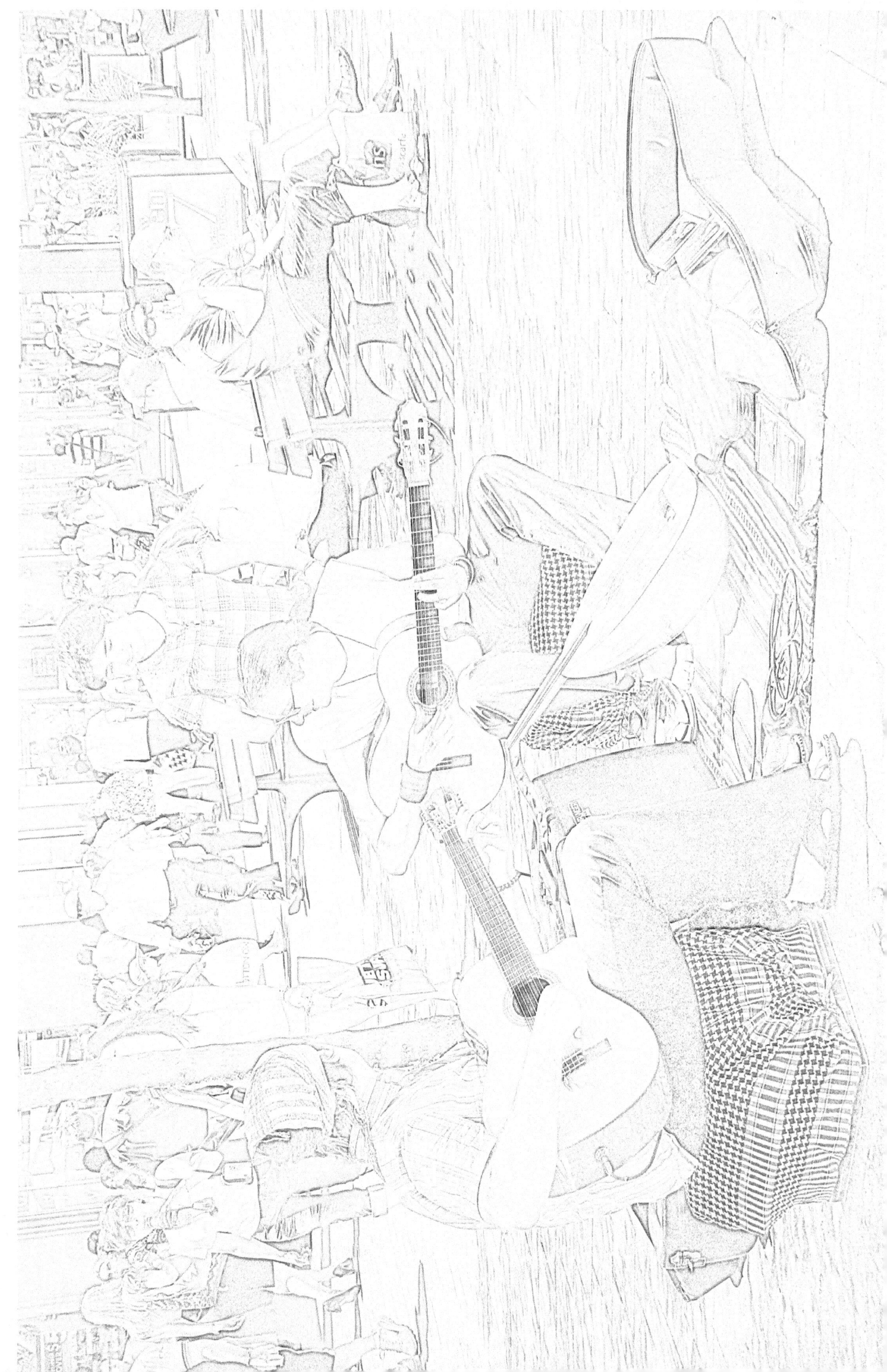

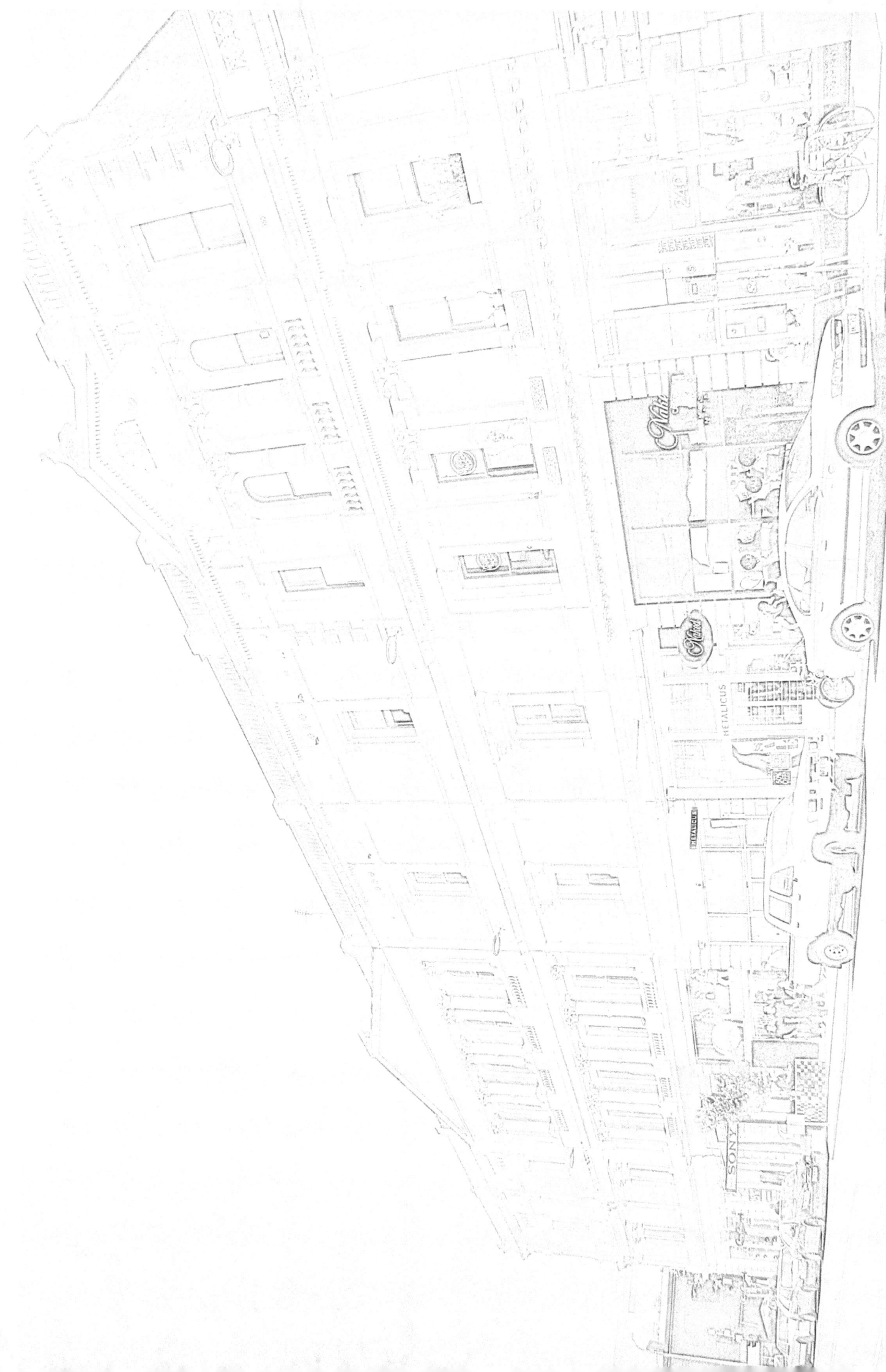

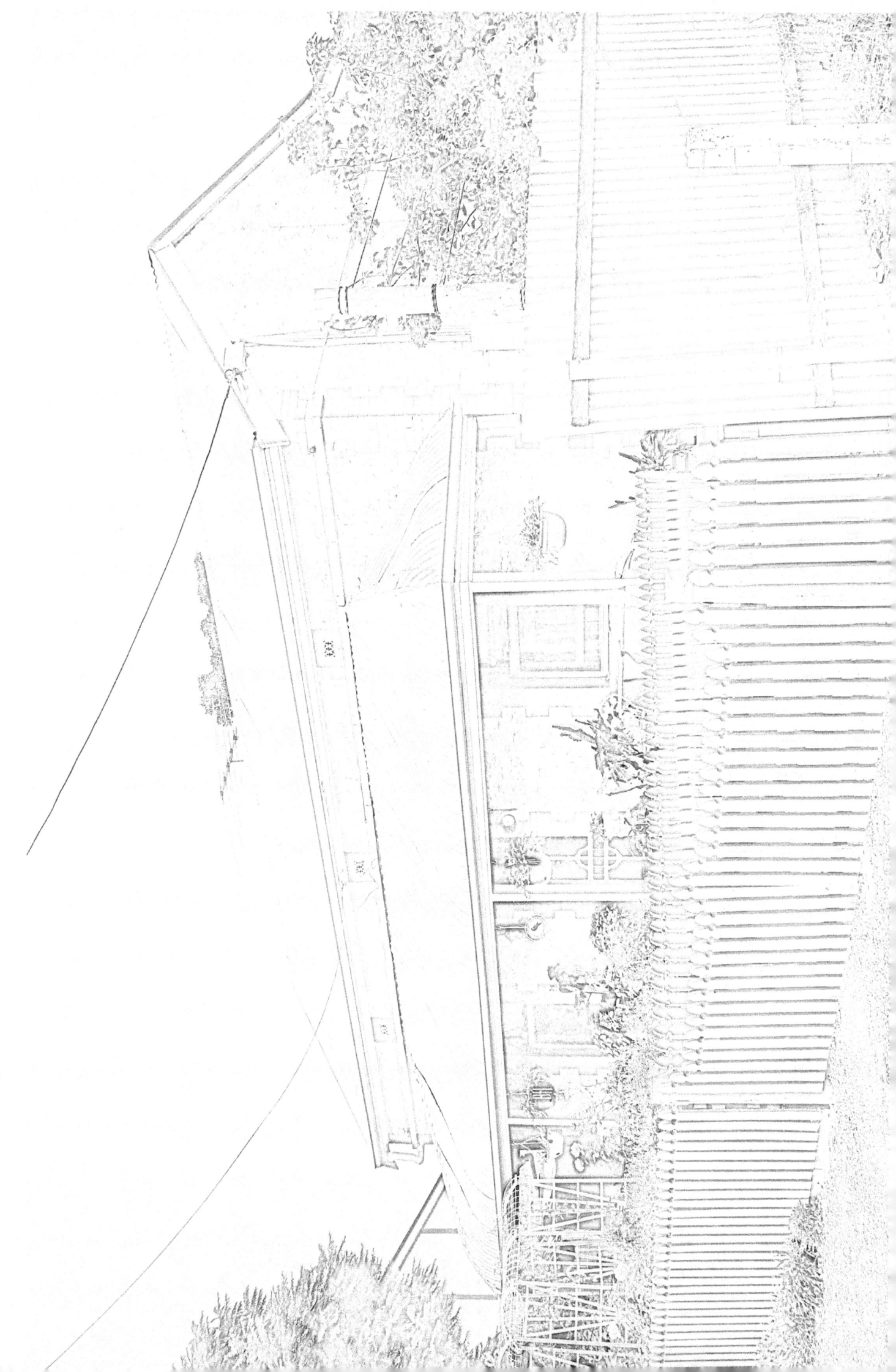

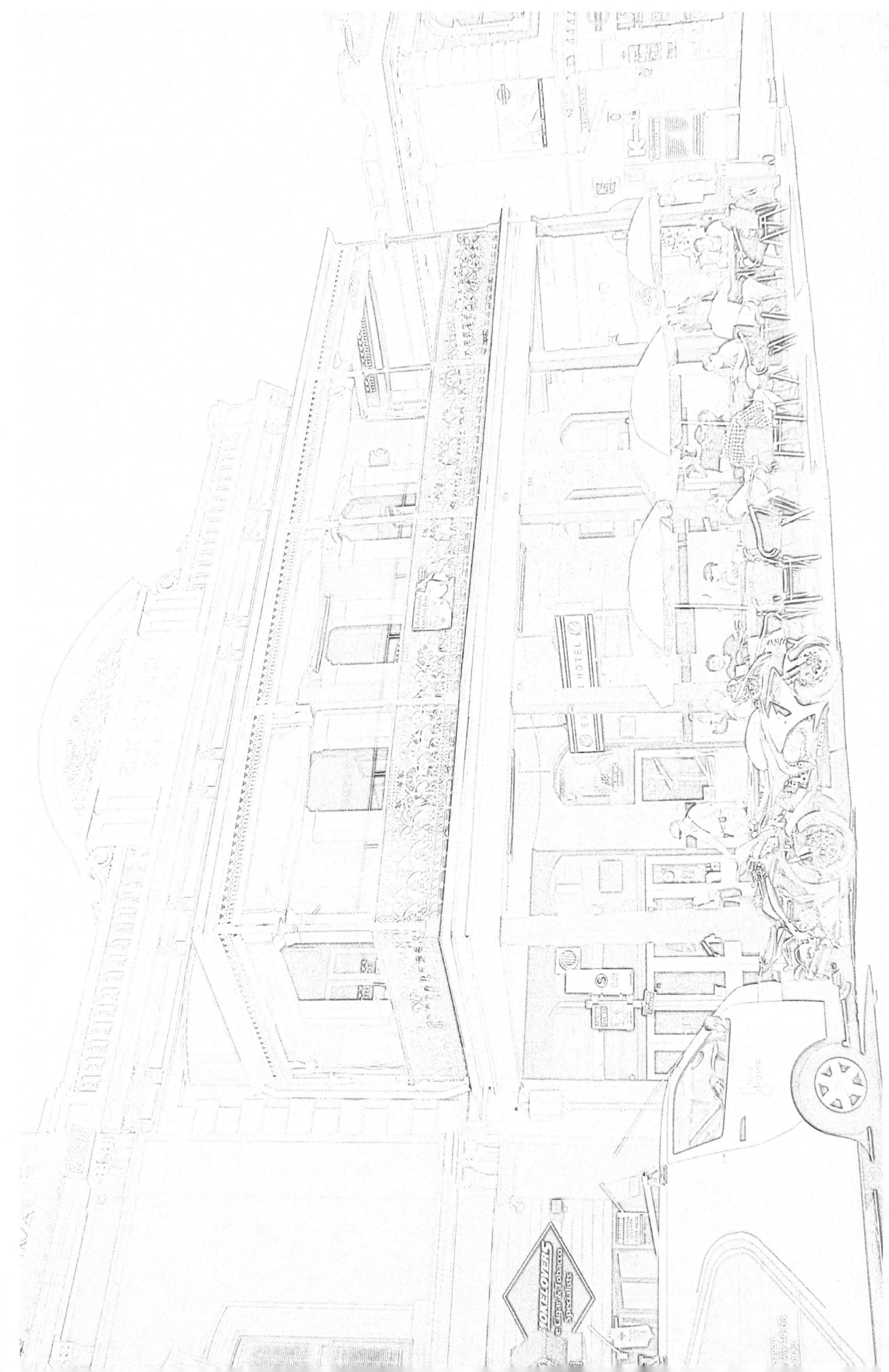